D1567640

The Anglican Chant Psalter

Edited by Alec Wyton

The Church Hymnal Corporation
445 Fifth Avenue, New York NY 10016

To the memory of Ray Brown
in gratitude for his great work
at The General Theological Seminary
and throughout the Church
until his death in 1965.

10   9   8   7   6   5

Contents

Preface

In the early 1930s the late Ray Francis Brown studied in England at the School of English Church Music (later the Royal School of Church Music) with Sir Sydney Nicholson. During this time he heard the psalms sung to the pointing of *The Parish Psalter*; this pointing is sometimes described as in "speech rhythm." Ray Brown returned to New York City to begin his legendary thirty-year tenure as Director of Music at The General Theological Seminary where he introduced this pointing in the chapel services. His manuscripts were tested not only in the Seminary Chapel but also in workshops and parishes around the country. In 1949 the final version was published by the Oxford University Press as *The Oxford American Psalter*. This Psalter was soon introduced in many parishes, cathedrals and seminary chapels and has continued in use until the publication of *The Book of Common Prayer* 1979.

Ray Brown's principles have been followed by the Standing Commission on Church Music in pointing the canticles and invitatory psalms in the *Hymnal 1982* and the psalms in this book. The intent is to bring to Anglican chanting the flexibility and expressiveness of well-modulated speech. Directions for chanting are suggested on a later page.

Frederick Burgomaster, Scott Cantrell, Franklin Coleman, Richard Wayne Dirksen, John Fenstermaker, Raymond F. Glover, Gerre Hancock, David Hurd, The Rev. Christopher P. Kelley, David Koehring, James Litton, Douglas Major, Murray Somerville and Herbert Tinney helped enormously in the selection of chants and testing of the pointing. In this book, the first setting to each psalm is considered congregational and the second choral.

The Standing Commission on Church Music is grateful to all who have given help and advice and hopes that the singing of psalms may become more widespread in the worship of the church.

Introduction

The Anglican Chant Psalter provides congregations and choirs with a method of singing the psalms using Anglican chant; this method underlies the sense of the words and the rhythm of well-modulated speech.

Psalms are hymns or songs. The *Harvard Dictionary of Music* says, "In their original form the psalms were not pure poetry but songs, perhaps with instrumental accompaniment." Following the authorization of *The Book of Common Prayer* 1979, with its restoration of psalms in the Eucharist, the practice of singing the psalms has grown in churches in the United States. Singing leads to a unanimity of sound or utterance which is seldom found in reading and thus provides a corporate expression which is at the heart of public worship.

Ray Brown in his introduction to *The Oxford American Psalter* speaks of chant as:

> "a development of the monotone. . .Plain chant came first. It was related to the musical pattern of the age in which it originated. The Anglican chant came much later and is related to the modern musical pattern. . .A psalm chant (Anglican or Gregorian) is a short, simple, flexible piece of music for the singing of unmetrical poetry, especially the psalms and canticles, in such a manner that the free, irregular rhythm of the words can be preserved in the singing. . ."

In the Psalter each verse is divided by an asterisk (*). The first syllable or syllables of each line are monotoned on the first note of the chant until the sign (ꞌ) indicates that the second and third notes of the chant are now sung. Two or more syllables sung to one note are indicated by a bracket (⌐⌐) and when one syllable is sung to two notes the indication is two dots (••). The next (ꞌ) indicates that the fourth note of the chant is now sung. Occasionally the reciting (or monotoned) note is omitted and this is indicated at the beginning of a line in the following way: "—ꞌeverything theyꞌdo shallꞌprosper." A breath is usually taken at the asterisk. A breath is usually taken also at the end of a line [unless the sense of the words suggests that the lines be continuous.] Rhetorical commas but not grammatical ones are observed as the sense would require in good reading. A dagger (†) indicates that a verse is sung to the second half of a double chant. The syllable "ed" at the end of a word is not to be pronounced separately except in obvious cases like "regarded" and "blessed."

Professor Brown in his introduction speaks helpfuly and practically about chanting:
> "Good monotoning is the basis of good chanting, but good monotoning is not to be had without attention and practice. The three steps in learning to chant a verse in good style are: (1) reading, (2) monotoning, and (3) chanting. After the standard of intelligibility has been set by deliberate reading, monotoning seems easy, but its apparent simplicity is deceiving.

> "The reason it requires so much attention is that in singing, as compared with speaking, the tone is more sustained, and the vowels generally are lengthened; but actually, singers without training in this will clip certain syllables of primary accent, with the result that they fail to take their proper stress. Syllables most likely to suffer this fault are those with short vowels and those ending in l, m, n, or v. The remedy is simply to lengthen such syllables just enough so that they will take the stress required by the sense of the words. The best way to deal with the syllables ending in these consonants is to delay the pronunciation of the consonants enough to give the vowel a chance to take its stress. (Examples: let, lips; soul, come, son, love; fill, him, sin, sing, live.).

> Another serious fault peculiar to singing consists in giving a strong accent to a final weak syllable whenever such a syllable occurs at a point where a break is made for breath, as at the end of a verse or half verse. This distortion of sound and sense plagues all singing, whether it be monotoning, Anglican chanting, Gregorian chanting, or any other form of vocal music, and whatever language is used; but the first and best place to be aware of it and correct it is in

monotoning. A final weak syllable (or note) is called a ["weak"]. . .ending. In English about half of all phrases and sentences have. . .such endings, and it is of the utmost importance that its natural gracefulness should be preserved in chanting. The first or second syllable preceding the weak ending always takes either a primary or a secondary stress, and the first step in correcting the fault is to see that the strong syllable is given its proper stress. The weak syllable should be lengthened slightly to prevent it from becoming inaudible and to add to the gracefulness of the termination. A final secondary accent, also, must be subordinated to the preceding primary accent: "Worship the Lord in the ˈbeauty of ˈholiness." There is no difficulty with. . .strong endings. It should be realized that, when the distinction between strong and weak endings is brought out, a lovely sort of variety is given to this music which is so often accused of being monotonous.

"Certain other faults common to speaking and singing can best be corrected by giving attention to monotoning. Articulation of consonants should be made very clear. Words of three or more syllables should be pronounced fully and deliberately and not snapped out (heartily, righteousness, enemies). When vowels occur in juxtaposition as 'we are' and 'he is,' they must not be allowed to merge; and when the first is stronger than the second, the tendency to move the accent from the first to the second must be withstood. A comma should be observed by prolonging the preceding syllable enough to make the sense clear (but its length should not be more than doubled), and not by a choppy break in the flow or the words. When two strong syllables are in juxtaposition, the first of the two should be lengthened ('great King'). When a weak syllable comes at the end of a recitation, just before the inflection begins, care must be taken not to lengthen or emphasize it at all ("For the Lord is a ˈgreat ˈGod").

"The pace of the recitation is determined by the two opposing requirements of clarity and fluency; on the one hand, all details of pronunciation should be explicit with pure vowels, clear consonants, and right accentuation; and on the other hand, the movement should be quick and flexible. Attention to clarity will keep the tempo from being too fast, and attention to fluency will keep it from being too slow.

"In English the vowels are not all of equal length. If the foregoing principles, especially the careful pronunciation of consonants, are observed in chanting, the syllables will be more nearly equal in duration than they are in normal speech. But the syllables should not be made exactly equal in duration, as is sometimes wrongly done in plainsong psalm chanting in English."

(From The Oxford American Psalter *by Ray F. Brown. Copyright 1949 by Ray F. Brown; renewed 1976 by Andrew Brown and Stuart Brown. Reprinted by permission of Oxford University Press, Inc.)*

Dr. Brown's introduction has been quoted at length because it is to the point and the singing in the chapel at The General Theological Seminary reflected his careful teaching.

Anglican Chant was designed to be sung in four-part harmony unless specifically indicated otherwise. In this book each psalm is given two chants. The first is intended for congregational use and the second for use by a carefully trained choir. In some parishes it may be possible for the congregation to sing certain choral chants, especially after having heard them sung by the choir several times. When a church has such a choir a psalm may be sung to either the first or second setting as a short anthem or during the communion of the people at the Eucharist or perhaps as a prelude to the service. The work of contemporary composers is well represented in this volume.

In accompanying chant the accompaniment serves to maintain pitch. Rhythmic leadership must come from the singers. The organ registers for Anglican Chant should be clear but unobtrusive and 16-foot pedal tone should be sparingly used. If choir and congregation are very secure in their singing, the accompanist may improvise descant forms of the chant or occasionally leave the voices unaccompanied. The accompaniment, as indeed the dynamics of the singing, may reflect the changing mood and meaning of the psalm but should at all costs avoid becoming theatrical.

Alec Wyton
New York City, February 1, 1985

Performance Notes

Singing the Chant

Good chanting is good singing. Chant is a musical medium for the clear and expressive singing of liturgical texts. Word accents create the rhythm in chant, and the lines and verses of the text determine the shape of the chant's musical phrase. Single-line melodic chant should be sung as song, whether lyrical or declamatory, as the words require. Harmonized chant is best sung with the same care one would give to the singing of harmonized folk or art song, with constant attention to the rhythm and phrasing of the text.

In singing all chant, special attention must be paid to the words sung to the reciting note or chord. The recitation must not be rushed and should be governed by the rhythm and flow of the words. Mediant cadences (the musical change at mid-point) and final endings or cadences should never slow down or speed up, creating a false metrical effect. The established and recurring tempo of the recitation remains the same throughout the chant, including the intonation, reciting notes, and the mediant and final cadences. On the other hand, the text is not to be sung with a mechanical, unbending pulse. Certain words will be gently moved along; others will be prolonged. Care is to be taken, however, not to sing the text with unnatural dotted rhythms.

Unaccented words or syllables at the beginning of lines should be treated as anacrustic, moving directly to the first primary accent. In general, accents should be created by lengthening the word or syllable (agogic accent) rather than by a sudden dynamic stress. Tempo and dynamics are to be determined by the meaning of the text, the number of singers, and the size and resonance of the space where they are singing.

If singers read the text in an expressive but not exaggerated manner, and then sing the words to the chant with the same rhythmic flow, they will discover how chant can unify the Christian community's singing of liturgical texts.

Harmonized (Anglican) Chant

The chant known as anglican chant developed from harmonized plainsong psalm tones (fauxbourdon) and from festal psalm settings by late sixteenth and early seventeenth century English composers. During the following centuries the daily singing of Prayer Book psalms to anglican chant became normal practice in English cathedrals, collegiate churches and chapels, and in many parish churches. Anglican chant psalm singing is still widely practiced throughout the Anglican Communion. The singing of the invitatory psalm and canticles to anglican chant became a widespread practice in the Episcopal Church and remains popular in many parishes.

A single chant is usually composed of ten chords—a reciting chord followed by a mediant cadence of three chords, and a second reciting chord followed by five chords which make up the final cadence or ending. The chant thus reflects the usual parallel construction of the canticles or psalms. The first half of each verse is sung to the first part of the chant. The second reciting chord and final cadence carry the remainder of the text following the asterisk. A double chant is twice as long, and two verses of a canticle or psalm are sung to double chants. *The Anglican Chant Psalter* also includes some triple chants.

Because of its fixed design, anglican chant requires the text to be marked ("pointed"), so that certain syllables may be sung to particular notes of the music. The pointing used in *The Anglican Chant Psalter* matches primary verbal stresses with musical ones. Musical stress is assumed to occur on the second, fourth, sixth, eighth, and tenth chords of the chant:

Syllable of primary stress have been, in most cases, assigned to these chords. This results in endings of varying lengths. Such endings add diversity to the chanting experience. They also invite fuller participation by congregations and choirs who will find their singing more consistent with their speaking.

Five marks indicate the pointing:

[|] always occurs before a stressed syllable to be sung to the second, fourth, sixth, eighth, and tenth chords of the chant. Thus its placement corresponds to the bar lines in the chant.

⌐‾‾‾¬ connects two syllables (occasionally three) to be sung to one chord.

¨ identifies one syllable to be sung to two chords.

— indicates that the reciting chord is to be omitted.

† indicates that the second half of a double chant is to be sung to this verse. When occurring during the use of a triple chant, indicates the use of the third section.

The musical notation is purely conventional and defines pitch but not duration. The notes have no rhythmic value in themselves and the text alone determines the rhythm. In the past the usual notation was in whole and half notes, with passing notes, when included, notated in quarter notes. *The Anglican Chant Psalter* uses half and quarter notes (with passing notes as eighth notes), providing greater ease in reading.

Passing notes (see chants #12, #143 and #281) may be treated in either of the following ways:

1. The last syllable before the bar line is always assigned to the passing notes, or
2. When the last syllable before the bar line is accented it is sung to the passing note, but when it is unaccented, the first syllable following the bar line is anticipated and the passing note is slurred to the following note.

Breath is always taken at the end of a line and after a colon or semi-colon in the middle of a line. A comma is always observed only as required in good reading and not by a complete break.

When singing anglican chant settings of canticles and psalms, particular care should be taken to make sure that the rhythm, sense, and mood of the words govern the tempo, dynamics, and style of the singing. At no time should the harmonic rhythm of the mediant cadence and ending be superimposed on the natural flow of the text. Care must be taken to guard against rushing words sung to reciting chords and slowing down to a measured rhythm at the mediant cadence and at the ending. Even though anglican chant developed as a medium for the four part choral singing of the psalms, many congregations have found that the singing of canticles and psalms to anglican chant is practical and gratifying. While the usual practice is for the congregation to sing the melody of the chant in unison, part singing is strongly encouraged. The choir, organ, or other instruments lead by singing and playing all four parts with an occasional verse in unison. Some contemporary chants are written to be sung in unison supported by the instrumental accompaniment.

The organ is the normal instrument for the accompaniment of anglican chant, but other keyboard instruments may be used. It is possible to add an occasional instrumental or choral descant to some chants. All parts are to be played. The accompanist should memorize the chant so that complete attention can be given to the words. Organ registrations should be firm, but not overwhelming. The organ should provide adequate support for congregational singing without obscuring the articulation of the text. Reeds and other color stops may add dramatic emphasis in certain verses. The pedal is used, especially for congregational singing, but may be omitted in some verses, all four parts being played on the manuals only. When congregation and choir are singing securely and confidently, it is refreshing to have appropriate verses sung unaccompanied.

When use of the Gloria Patri is indicated by *The Book of Common Prayer,* it should be sung to the last chant used in a particular setting, except where noted otherwise. The following pointing for Gloria Patri may be used.

Glory to the Father, and ' to the ' Son, *
    and ' to the ' Holy ' Spirit:

As it was in the be ' ginning, is ' now, *
    and ' will be for ' ever. A ' men.

Concerning the Psalter

The Psalter is a body of liturgical poetry. It is designed for vocal, congregational use, whether by singing or reading. There are several traditional methods of psalmody. The exclusive use of a single method makes the recitation of the Psalter needlessly monotonous. The traditional methods, each of which can be elaborate or simple, are the following:

Direct recitation denotes the reading or chanting of a whole psalm, or portion of a psalm, in unison. It is particularly appropriate for the psalm verses suggested in the lectionary for use between the Lessons at the Eucharist, when the verses are recited rather than sung, and may often be found a satisfactory method of chanting them.

Antiphonal recitation is the verse-by-verse alternation between groups of singers or readers; *e.g.*, between choir and congregation, or between one side of the congregation and the other. The alternate recitation concludes either with the Gloria Patri, or with a refrain (called the antiphon) recited in unison. This is probably the most satisfying method for reciting the psalms in the Daily Office.

Responsorial recitation is the name given to a method of psalmody in which the verses of a psalm are sung by a solo voice, with the choir and the congregation singing a refrain after each verse or group of verses. This was the traditional method of singing the Venite, and the restoration of Invitatory Antiphons for the Venite makes possible a recovery of this form of sacred song in the Daily Office. It was also a traditional manner of chanting the psalms between the Lessons at the Eucharist, and it is increasingly favored by modern composers.

Responsive recitation is the method which has been most frequently used in Episcopal churches, the minister alternating with the congregation, verse by verse.

The version of the Psalms which follows is set out in lines of Poetry. The lines correspond to Hebrew versification, which is not based on meter or rhyme, but on parallelism of clauses, a symmetry of form and sense. The parallelism can take the form of similarity (The waters have lifted up, O Lord/the waters have lifted up their voice;/the waters have lifted up their pounding waves. *Psalm 93:4*), or of contrast (The Lord knows the ways of the righteous;/but the way of the wicked is doomed. *Psalm 1:6*) or of logical expansion (Our eyes look to the Lord our God,/ until he show us his mercy. *Psalm 123:3*).

The most common verse is a couplet, but triplets are very frequent, and quatrains are not unknown; although quatrains are usually distributed over two verses.

An asterisk divides each verse into two parts for reading or chanting. In reading, a distinct pause should be made at the asterisk.

Three terms are used in the Psalms with referece to God: *Elohim* ("God"), *Adonai* ("Lord") and the personal name *YHWH*. The "Four-letter Name" (Tetragrammaton) is probably to be vocalized Yahweh; but this is by no means certain, because from very ancient times it has been considered too sacred to be pronounced; and, whenever it occurred, *Adonai* was substituted for it. In the oldest manuscripts, the Divine Name was written in antique and obsolete letters; in more recent manuscripts and in printed Bibles, after the invention of vowel points, the Name was provided with the vowels of the word *Adonai*. This produced a hybrid form which has been translated "Jehovah."

The Hebrew reverence and reticence with regard to the Name of God has been carried over into the classical English versions, the Prayer Book Psalter and the King James Old Testament, where it is regularly rendered "Lord." In order to distinguish it, however, from "Lord" as a translation of *Adonai*, *YHWH* is represented in capital and small capital letters: LORD.

From time to time, the Hebrew text has *Adonai* and *YHWH* in conjunction. Then, the Hebrew custom is to substitute *Elohim* for *YHWH,* and our English translation follows suit, rendering the combined title as "Lord GOD."

In two passages (*Psalm 68:4* and *Psalm 83:18*), the context requires that the Divine Name be spelled out, and it appears as YAHWEH. A similar construction occurs in the Canticle, "The Song of Moses."

The ancient praise-shout, "Hallelujah," has been restored, in place of its English equivalent, "Praise the Lord." The Hebrew form has been used, rather than the Latin form "Alleluia," as being more appropriate to this context; but also to regain for our liturgy a form of the word that is familiar from its use in many well-known anthems. The word may, if desired, be omitted during the season of Lent.

The Anglican Chant Psalter

Psalm 1 *Beatus vir qui non abiit*

1 Happy are they who have not walked in the ⌐counsel of the ⌐wicked, *
  nor lingered in the way of sinners,
  nor ⌐sat in the ⌐seats of the ⌐scornful!

2 Their delight is in the ⌐law of the ⌐LORD, *
  and they meditate on his ⌐läw ⌐day and ⌐night.

3 They are like trees planted by streams of water,
  bearing fruit in due season, with leaves that ⌐do not ⌐wither; *
  — ⌐everything they ⌐do shall prosper.

4 It is not ⌐so with the ⌐wicked; *
  they are like ⌐chaff which the ⌐wind blows a ⌐way.

5 Therefore the wicked shall not stand upright when ⌐judgment ⌐comes, *
  nor the sinner in the ⌐council ⌐of the ⌐righteous.

6 For the LORD knows the ⌐way of the ⌐righteous, *
  but the ⌐way of the ⌐wicked is ⌐doomed.

Psalm 2 *Quare fremuerunt gentes?*

3   *Edwin George Monk*

4   *Bryan Hesford*

1 Why are the ˈnations in an ˈuproar? *
   Why do the peoples ˈmutter ˈempty ˈthreats?

2 Why do the kings of the earth rise up in revolt,
   and the princes ˈplot to ˈgether, *
   against the ˈLORD and a ˈgainst his A ˈnointed?

3 "Let us break their ˈyoke," they ˈsay; *
   "let us cast ˈoff their ˈbonds ˈfrom us."

4 He whose throne is in ˈheaven is ˈlaughing; *
   the Lord ˈhas them ˈin de ˈrision.

5 Then he speaks to ˈthem in his ˈwrath, *
   and his ˈrage ˈfills them with ˈterror.

6 "I myself have ˈset my ˈking *
   upon my ˈholy ˈhill of ˈZion."

7 Let me announce the de ˈcree of the ˈLORD: *
   he said to me, "You are my Son;
   this day ˈhave ˈI be ˈgotten you.

8 Ask of me, and I will give you the nations for ˈyour in ˈheritance *
   and the ends of the ˈearth for ˈyour pos ˈsession.

†9 You shall crush them with an'iron'rod *
   and shatter them'like a'piece of'pottery."

10 And now, you'kings, be'wise; *
   be warned, you'rulers'of the'earth.

11 Submit to the'LORD with'fear, *
   and with'trembling'bow be'fore him;

12 Lest he be'angry and you'perish; *
   for his'wrath is'quickly'kindled.

13 Happy'are they'all *
   —'who take'refuge in'him!

Psalm 3   *Domine, quid multiplicati*

5   Jonathan Battishill

6   Richard Coulson

1 LORD, how many'adversaries I'have! *
   how many there are who'rise'up a'gainst me!

2 How many there'are who'say of me, *
   "There is no'help for him'in his'God."

3 But you, O LORD, are a'shield a'bout me; *
   you are my glory, the'one who lifts'up my'head.

4 I call aloud up'on the'LORD, *
   and he answers me'from his'holy'hill;

3

5

Jonathan Battishill

6

Richard Coulson

5 I lie down and ' go to ' sleep; *
I wake again, be ' cause the ' LORD sus ' tains me.

6 I do not fear the ' multitudes of ' people *
who set themselves a ' gainst me ' all a ' round.

7 Rise up, O LORD; set me ' free, O my ' God; *
surely, you will strike all my enemies across the face,
you will ' break the ' teeth of the ' wicked.

8 Deliverance be ' longs to the ' LORD. *
Your blessing ' be up ' on your ' people!

Psalm 4   *Cum invocarem*

7

William Knyvett (after Handel)

8

John Joubert

1 Answer me when I call, O God, de'fender of my 'cause; *
   you set me free when I am hard-pressed;
   have mercy on 'me and 'hear my 'prayer.

2 "You mortals, how long will you dis'honor my 'glory; *
   how long will you worship dumb idols
   and 'run after false 'gods?"

3 Know that the LORD does 'wonders for the 'faithful; *
   when I call upon the 'LORD, 'he will 'hear me.

4 Tremble, then, and 'do not 'sin; *
   speak to your heart in 'silence up'on your 'bed.

5 Offer the ap'pointed 'sacrifices *
   and 'put your 'trust in the 'LORD.

6 Many are saying,
   "Oh, that we might see 'better 'times!" *
   Lift up the light of your 'countenance up'on us, O 'LORD.

7 You have put 'gladness in my 'heart, *
   more than when grain and 'wine and 'oil in'crease.

8 I lie down in peace; at once I 'fall a'sleep; *
   for only you, LORD, 'make me 'dwell in 'safety.

5

Psalm 5   *Verba mea auribus*

9

Stephen Elvey

10

Thomas Attwood Walmisley

1 Give ear to my ˈwords, O ˈLORD; *
   conˈsider my ˈmediˈtation.

2 Hearken to my cry for help, my ˈKing and my ˈGod, *
   for I ˈmake my ˈprayer to ˈyou.

3 In the morning, LORD, you ˈhear my ˈvoice; *
   early in the morning I ˈmake my apˈpeal and ˈwatch for you.

4 For you are not a God who takes ˈpleasure in ˈwickedness, *
   and ˈevil ˈcannot ˈdwell with you.

5 Braggarts cannot ˈstand in your ˈsight; *
   you hate all ˈthose who ˈwörk ˈwickedness.

6 You destroy ˈthose who speak ˈlies; *
   the bloodthirsty and deceitful, O ˈLÖRD, ˈyou abˈhor.

†7 But as for me, through the greatness of your mercy I
      will ˈgo into your ˈhouse; *
   I will bow down toward your ˈholy ˈtemple in ˈawe of you.

8 Lead me, O LORD, in your righteousness,
   because of those who ˈlie in ˈwait for me; *
   make your ˈwäy ˈstraight beˈfore me.

9 For there is no ⌐truth in their ⌐mouth; *
  there is de⌐struction ⌐in their ⌐heart;

10 Their throat is an ⌐open ⌐grave; *
  they ⌐flatter ⌐with their ⌐tongue.

11 Declare them ⌐guilty, O ⌐God; *
  let them ⌐fall, be⌐cause of their ⌐schemes.

12 Because of their many transgressions ⌐cast them ⌐out, *
  for ⌐they have re⌐belled a⌐gainst you.

13 But all who take refuge in ⌐you will be ⌐glad; *
  they will sing ⌐out their ⌐joy for ⌐ever.

14 — ⌐You will ⌐shelter them, *
  so that those who love your ⌐Näme ⌐may ex⌐ult in you.

15 For you, O LORD, will ⌐bless the ⌐righteous; *
  you will defend them with your ⌐favor as ⌐with a ⌐shield.

Psalm 6 *Domine, ne in furore*

11   *John Goss*

12   *John Goss*

1 LORD, do not re'buke me in your'anger; *
 do not'punish me'in your'wrath.

2 Have pity on me, LORD, for'I am'weak; *
 heal me,'LORD, for my'bones are'racked.

3 My spirit'shakes with'terror; *
 how'long, O'LORD, how'long?

4 Turn, O'LORD, and de'liver me; *
 —'save me for your'mercy's'sake.

5 For in death'no one re'members you; *
 and who will'give you'thanks in the'grave?

6 I grow weary be'cause of my'groaning; *
 every night I drench my bed
 and'flood my'couch with'tears.

8

7 My eyes are ˈwasted with ˈgrief *
  and worn away beˈcause of ˈall my ˈenemies.

8 Depart from me, all ˈevil ˈdoers, *
  for the LORD has ˈheard the ˈsound of my ˈweeping.

9 The LORD has ˈheard my suppliˈcation; *
  the ˈLORD acˈcepts my ˈprayer.

10 All my enemies shall be confounded and ˈquake with ˈfear; *
  they shall turn back and ˈsuddenly be ˈput to ˈshame.

Psalm 7 *Domine, Deus meus*

13

James Turle

14

Richard Farrant

1 O LORD my God, I take ˈrefuge in ˈyou; *
  save and deˈliver me from ˈall who purˈsue me;

2 Lest like a lion they ˈtear me in ˈpieces *
  and snatch me aˈway with ˈnone to deˈliver me.

3 O LORD my God, if I have ˈdone these ˈthings: *
  if there is any ˈwickedness ˈin my ˈhands,

4 If I have repaid my ˈfriend with ˈevil, *
  or plundered him who without ˈcaüse ˈis my ˈenemy;

9

13

James Turle

14

Richard Farrant

5 Then let my enemy pursue and 'over'take me, *
    trample my life into the ground,
    and lay my 'honor 'in the 'dust.

6 Stand up, O 'LORD, in your 'wrath; *
    rise up against the 'fury 'of my 'enemies.

7 Awake, O my God, de'crëe 'justice; *
    let the assembly of the 'peoples 'gather 'round you.

8 Be seated on your lofty 'throne, O Most 'High; *
    O 'LÖRD, 'judge the 'nations.

9 Give judgment for me according to my 'righteousness, O 'LORD, *
    and according to my 'innocence, 'O Most 'High.

10 Let the malice of the wicked come to an end,
    but es'tablish the 'righteous; *
    for you test the mind and 'heart, O 'righteous 'God.

11 God is my 'shield and de'fense; *
    he is the 'savior of the 'true in 'heart.

12 God is a 'righteous 'judge; *
    God sits in 'judgment 'every 'day.

13 If they will not repent, God will 'whet his 'sword; *
    he will bend his 'bow and 'make it 'ready.

14 He has prepared his 'weapons of 'death; *

    he makes his 'arrows 'shafts of 'fire.

15 Look at those who are in 'labor with 'wickedness, *

    who conceive evil, and give 'birth 'to a 'lie.

16 They dig a pit and 'make it 'deep *

    and fall into the 'hole that 'they have 'made.

17 Their malice turns back upon their 'own 'head; *

    their violence 'falls on 'their own 'scalp.

18 I will bear witness that the 'LORD is 'righteous; *

    I will praise the 'Name of the 'LORD Most 'High.

Psalm 8   *Domine, Dominus noster*

15   *Ivor Keys*

16   *William Henry Harris*

1 O 'LORD our 'Governor, *

    how exalted is your 'Name in 'all the 'world!

2 Out of the mouths of 'infants and 'children *

    your majesty is 'praised a'bove the 'heavens.

3 You have set up a stronghold a'gainst your 'adversaries, *

    to quell the 'enemy 'and the a'venger.

4 When I consider your heavens, the 'work of your 'fingers, *

    the moon and the 'stars you have 'set in their 'courses,

15   *Ivor Keys*

16   *William Henry Harris*

5 What is man that you should be ⌐mindful of⌐him? *
    the son of man that⌐you should⌐seek him⌐out?

6 You have made him but little⌐lower than the⌐angels; *
    you a⌐dorn him with⌐glory and⌐honor;

7 You give him mastery over the⌐works of your⌐hands; *
    you put⌐all things⌐under his⌐feet:

8 All⌐sheep and⌐oxen, *
    even the wild⌐beästs⌐of the⌐field,

9 The birds of the air, the⌐fish of the⌐sea, *
    and whatsoever⌐walks in the⌐paths of the⌐sea.

10 O⌐LORD our⌐Governor, *
    how exalted is your⌐Name in⌐all the⌐world!

Psalm 9 *Confitebor tibi*

17

Henry Edward Dibdin

18

Joseph Pring

1 I will give thanks to you, O LORD, with my ' whŏle ' heart; *
    I will tell of ' all your ' marvelous ' works.

2 I will be ' glad and re ' joice in you; *
    I will sing to your ' Näme, ' O Most ' High.

3 When my enemies are ' driven ' back, *
    they will stumble and ' perish ' at your ' presence.

4 For you have maintained my ' right and my ' cause; *
    you sit upon your ' thrŏne ' judging ' right.

5 You have rebuked the ungodly and des ' troyed the ' wicked; *
    you have blotted out their ' name for ' ever and ' ever.

6 As for the enemy, they are finished, in per ' petual ' ruin, *
    their cities plowed under, the ' memory ' of them ' perished;

7 But the LORD is en ' throned for ' ever; *
    he has set ' up his ' throne for ' judgment.

8 It is he who rules the ' world with ' righteousness; *
    he ' judges the ' peoples with ' equity.

13

17

Henry Edward Dibdin

18

Joseph Pring

9 The LORD will be a refuge|for the op|pressed, *
   a|refuge in|time of|trouble.

10 Those who know your Name will|put their|trust in you, *
   for you never forsake|those who|seek you, O|LORD.

11 Sing praise to the LORD who|dwells in|Zion; *
   proclaim to the|peoples the|things he has|done.

12 The Avenger of|blood will re|member them; *
   he will not forget the|cry of|the af|flicted.

13 Have pity on|me, O|LORD; *
   see the misery I suffer from those who hate me,
   O you who lift me|up from the|gate of|death;

14 So that I may tell of all your praises
   and rejoice in|your sal|vation *
   in the|gates of the|city of|Zion.

15 The ungodly have fallen into the|pit they|dug, *
   and in the snare they|set is their|own foot|caught.

16 The LORD is known by his|acts of|justice; *
   the wicked are trapped in the|works of|their own|hands.

17 The wicked shall be given ⌐over to the⌐ grave, *
   and also all the ⌐peoples that for⌐gët⌐ God.

18 For the needy shall not ⌐always be for⌐gotten, *
   and the hope of the ⌐poor shall not ⌐perish for ⌐ever.

19 Rise up, O LORD, let not the ungodly have the ⌐upper ⌐hand; *
   — ⌐let them be ⌐judged be⌐fore you.

20 Put fear up⌐on them, O ⌐LORD; *
   let the ungodly ⌐know they ⌐are but ⌐mortal.

Psalm 10   *Ut quid, Domine?*

19   *Matthew Camidge*

20   *David Hurd*

1 Why do you stand so far ⌐off, O ⌐LORD, *
   and hide your⌐self in ⌐time of ⌐trouble?

2 The wicked arrogantly ⌐persecute the ⌐poor, *
   but they are trapped in the ⌐schemes they ⌐have de⌐vised.

3 The wicked boast of their ⌐heart's de⌐sire; *
   the covetous ⌐curse and re⌐vile the ⌐LORD.

4 The wicked are so proud that they ⌐care not for ⌐God; *
   their only ⌐thought is, ⌐"God does not ⌐matter."

19 *Matthew Camidge*

20 *David Hurd*

5 Their ways are devious at all times;
  your judgments are far above ⌐out of their⌐sight; *
    —⌐they defy⌐all their⌐enemies.

6 They say in their heart, "I shall⌐not be⌐shaken; *
  no harm shall⌐happen⌐to me⌐ever."

7 Their mouth is full of cursing, de⌐ceit, and op⌐pression; *
  under their⌐tongue are⌐mischief and⌐wrong.

8 They lurk in ambush in public squares
  and in secret places they⌐murder the⌐innocent; *
    they⌐spy⌐out the⌐helpless.

9 They lie in wait, like a lion in a covert;
  they lie in wait to⌐seize upon the⌐lowly; *
    they seize the lowly and⌐drag them a⌐way in their⌐net.

10 The innocent are broken and⌐humbled be⌐fore them; *
  the helpless⌐fall be⌐fore their⌐power.

†11 They say in their heart,⌐"God has for⌐gotten; *
  he hides his⌐face; he will⌐never⌐notice."

12 Rise up, O LORD;
  lift up your⌐hand, O⌐God; *
    do⌐not for⌐get the af⌐flicted.

16

13 Why should the wicked re'vile 'God? *
     why should they say in their 'heart, "You 'do not 'care"?

14 Surely, you behold 'trouble and 'misery; *
     you see it and take it 'into 'your own 'hand.

15 The helpless commit them'selves to 'you, *
     for 'you are the 'helper of 'orphans.

16 Break the power of the 'wicked and 'evil; *
     search out their wickedness un'til you 'find 'none.

17 The LORD is King for'ever and 'ever; *
     the ungodly shall 'perish 'from his 'land.

18 The LORD will hear the de'sire of the 'humble; *
     you will strengthen their 'heart and your 'ears shall 'hear;

19 To give justice to the 'orphan and op'pressed, *
     so that mere mortals may 'strike 'terror no 'more.

Psalm 11 *In Domino confido*

21

C. Hylton Stewart

22

David Hurd (after Gibbons)

1 In the LORD have I ˈtaken ˈrefuge; *
    how then can you say to me,
    "Fly aˈway like a ˈbird to the ˈhilltop;

2 For see how the wicked bend the bow
    and fit their ˈarrows to the ˈstring, *
    to shoot from ˈambush at the ˈtrue of ˈheart.

3 When the foundations are ˈbeing desˈtroyed, *
    —ˈwhat can the ˈrighteous ˈdo?"

4 The LORD is in his ˈholy ˈtemple; *
    the ˈLÖRD'S ˈthrone is in ˈheaven.

5 His eyes behold the inˈhabited ˈworld; *
    his piercing ˈeÿe ˈweighs our ˈworth.

6 The LORD weighs the righteous as ˈwell as the ˈwicked, *
    but those who delight in ˈviolence ˈhe abˈhors.

7 Upon the wicked he shall rain coals of fire and ˈburning ˈsulphur; *
    a scorching ˈwind shall ˈbe their ˈlot.

8 For the LORD is righteous;
    he delights in ˈrighteous ˈdeeds; *
    and the ˈjust shall ˈsee his ˈface.

Psalm 12   *Salvum me fac*

23

Richard Clark

24

Herbert Howells

1 Help me, LORD, for there is no ⌐godly one ⌐left; *
    the faithful have ⌐vanished ⌐from a ⌐mong us.

2 Everyone speaks ⌐falsely with his ⌐neighbor; *
    with a smooth tongue they ⌐speak from a ⌐double ⌐heart.

3 Oh, that the LORD would cut off all ⌐smöoth ⌐tongues, *
    and close the lips that ⌐utter ⌐pröud ⌐boasts!

4 Those who say, "With our ⌐tongue will we pre ⌐vail; *
    our lips are our own; ⌐who is ⌐lörd ⌐over us?"

5 "Because the needy are oppressed,
    and the poor cry ⌐out in ⌐misery, *
        I will rise up," says the LORD
        "and ⌐give them the ⌐help they ⌐long for."

6 The words of the LORD are ⌐püre ⌐words, *
    like silver refined from ore
    and purified ⌐seven times ⌐in the ⌐fire.

7 O ⌐LORD, watch ⌐over us *
    and save us from ⌐this gene ⌐ration for ⌐ever.

8 The wicked prowl on ⌐every ⌐side, *
    and that which is worthless is ⌐highly ⌐prized by ⌐everyone.

19

Psalm 13 *Usquequo, Domine?*

25 *Parisian Tone*

26 *Walter Parratt*

1 How long, O LORD?
   will you for'get me for 'ever? *
      how 'long will you 'hide your 'face from me?

2 How long shall I have perplexity in my mind,
   and grief in my heart, 'day after 'day? *
      how long shall my 'enemy 'triumph 'over me?

3 Look upon me and answer me, O 'LORD my 'God; *
      give light to my 'eyes, lest I 'sleep in 'death;

4 Lest my enemy say, "I have pre'vailed 'over him," *
      and my foes re'joice that 'I have 'fallen.

5 But I put my 'trust in your 'mercy; *
      my heart is joyful be'cause of your 'saving 'help.

6 I will sing to the LORD, for he has 'dealt with me 'richly; *
      I will praise the 'Name of the 'Lord Most 'High.

Psalm 14 *Dixit insipiens*

27

John Goss

28

James Turle

1 The fool has said in his heart, "There ˈis no ˈGod." *
  All are corrupt and commit abominable acts;
  there is ˈnone who does ˈany ˈgood.

2 The LORD looks down from heaven up ˈon us ˈall, *
  to see if there is any who is wise,
  if there is ˈone who ˈseeks after ˈGod.

3 Every one has proved faithless;
  all a ˈlike have turned ˈbad; *
  there is none who does ˈgöod; ˈno, not ˈone.

4 Have they no knowledge, all those ˈevil ˈdoers *
  who eat up my people like bread
  and do not ˈcall up ˈon the ˈLORD?

5 See how they ˈtremble with ˈfear, *
  because God is in the ˈcompany ˈof the ˈrighteous.

6 Their aim is to confound the ˈplans of the af ˈflicted, *
  but the ˈLÖRD ˈis their ˈrefuge.

†7 Oh, that Israel's deliverance would come ˈout of ˈZion! *
  when the LORD restores the fortunes of his people,
  Jacob will re ˈjoice and ˈIsrael be ˈglad.

21

Psalm 15   *Domine, quis habitabit?*

29   *James Nares*

30   *David Hurd*

1 LORD, who may ˈdwell in your ˈtabernacle? *
   who may abide upˈon your ˈholy ˈhill?

2 Whoever leads a blameless life and ˈdoes what is ˈright, *
   who ˈspeaks the ˈtruth from his ˈheart.

3 There is no guile upon his tongue;
   he does no ˈevil to his ˈfriend; *
      he does not heap conˈtempt upˈon his ˈneighbor.

4 In his sight the ˈwicked is reˈjected, *
   but he honors ˈthose who ˈfear the ˈLORD.

5 He has sworn to ˈdo no ˈwrong *
   and ˈdoes not take ˈback his ˈword.

6 He does not give his money in ˈhope of ˈgain, *
   nor does he take a ˈbribe aˈgainst the ˈinnocent.

†7 Whoever ˈdoes these ˈthings *
   shall ˈnever be ˈoverˈthrown.

22

Psalm 16 *Conserva me, Domine*

31   *Richard H. Pinwill Coleman*

32   *Edward Cuthbert Bairstow*

1 Protect me, O God, for I take ˈrefuge inˈyou; *
    I have said to the LORD, "You are my Lord,
    myˈgood aˈbove allˈother."

2 All my delight is upon the godly that areˈin theˈland, *
    upon those who areˈnoble aˈmong theˈpeople.

3 But those who run afterˈotherˈgods *
    shallˈhave theirˈtroublesˈmultiplied.

4 Their libations of blood Iˈwill notˈoffer, *
    nor take the names of theirˈgods upˈon myˈlips.

5 O LORD, you are myˈportion and myˈcup; *
    it isˈyou who upˈhold myˈlot.

6 My boundaries enclose aˈpleasantˈland; *
    indeed, Iˈhave aˈgoodlyˈheritage.

7 I will bless the LORD whoˈgives meˈcounsel; *
    my heart teaches me,ˈnightˈafterˈnight.

8 I have set the LORDˈalways beˈfore me; *
    because he is at myˈright hand I ˈshall notˈfall.

†9 My heart, therefore, is glad, and myˈspirit reˈjoices; *
    my bodyˈalso shallˈrest inˈhope.

31

Richard H. Pinwill Coleman

32

Edward Cuthbert Bairstow

10 For you will not abandon me⏐to the⏐grave, *
    nor let your⏐holy one⏐see the⏐Pit.

11 You will show me the⏐path of⏐life; *
    in your presence there is fullness of joy,
    and in your right hand are⏐pleasures for⏐ever⏐more.

Psalm 17   *Exaudi, Domine*

33   William Best

34   Herbert Howells

1 Hear my plea of innocence, O LORD;
   give ˈheed to my ˈcry; *
        listen to my prayer, which does not ˈcome from ˈlying ˈlips.

2 Let my vindication come ˈforth from your ˈpresence; *
        let your ˈeyes be ˈfixed on ˈjustice.

3 Weigh my heart, ˈsummon me by ˈnight, *
        melt me down; you will find ˈno im ˈpurity ˈin me.

4 I give no offense with my mouth as ˈothers ˈdo; *
        I have ˈheeded the ˈwords of your ˈlips.

5 My footsteps hold fast to the ˈways of your ˈlaw; *
        in your ˈpaths my ˈfeet shall not ˈstumble.

6 I call upon you, O God, for ˈyou will ˈanswer me; *
        incline your ear to ˈme and ˈhear my ˈwords.

†7 Show me your marvelous ˈloving ˈkindness, *
        O Savior of those who take refuge at your right hand
        from ˈthose who rise ˈup a ˈgainst them.

8 Keep me as the ˈapple of your ˈeye; *
        hide me under the ˈshadow ˈof your ˈwings,

9 From the ˈwicked who as ˈsault me, *
        from my deadly ˈenemies ˈwho sur ˈround me.

25

33

William Best

34

Herbert Howells

10 They have closed their 'heart to 'pity, *
  and their 'mouth speaks 'proud 'things.

11 They press me hard,
  'now they sur'round me, *
    watching how they may 'cast me 'to the 'ground,

12 Like a lion, 'greedy for its 'prey, *
  and like a young lion 'lurking in 'secret 'places.

13 Arise, O LORD; confront them and 'bring them 'down; *
  deliver me from the 'wicked 'by your 'sword.

14 Deliver me, O 'LORD, by your 'hand *
  from those whose portion in 'life is 'this 'world;

15 Whose bellies you 'fill with your 'treasure, *
  who are well supplied with children
  and 'leave their 'wealth to their 'little ones.

†16 But at my vindication I shall 'see your 'face; *
  when I awake, I shall be 'satisfied, be'holding your 'likeness.

Psalm 18: Part 1   *Diligam te, Domine*

35   *James Turle*

37   *Ivor Algernon Atkins*

Setting 1: #35–36; setting 2: #37–38.

1 I love you, O ׀ LORD my ׀ strength, *
     O LORD my stronghold, my ׀ cräg, ׀ and my ׀ haven.

2 My God, my rock in whom I ׀ put my ׀ trust, *
     my shield, the horn of my salvation, and my refuge;
     ׀ you are ׀ worthy of ׀ praise.

†3 I will ׀ call upon the ׀ LORD, *
     and so shall I be ׀ saved ׀ from my ׀ enemies.

4 The breakers of ׀ death rolled ׀ over me, *
     and the torrents of ob ׀ livion ׀ made me a ׀ fraid.

5 The cords of ׀ hell en ׀ tangled me, *
     and the ׀ snares of ׀ death were ׀ set for me.

6 I called upon the LORD in ׀ my dis ׀ tress *
     and cried ׀ out to my ׀ God for ׀ help.

7 He heard my voice from his ׀ heavenly ׀ dwelling; *
     my cry of ׀ anguish ׀ came to his ׀ ears.

27

35

James Turle

37

Ivor Algernon Atkins

8 The earth'reeled and'rocked; *
  they roots of the mountains shook;
  they'reeled be'cause of his'anger.

9 Smoke rose from his nostrils
  and a consuming fire'out of his'mouth; *
  hot burning'cöals'blazed forth'from him.

10 He parted the heavens and'cäme'down *
   with a'storm cloud'under his'feet.

11 He mounted on'cherubim and'flew; *
   he'swooped on the'wings of the'wind.

†12 He wrapped'darkness a'bout him; *
   he made dark waters and thick'clöuds'his pa'vilion.

13 From the brightness of his'presence, through the'clouds, *
   burst'hailstones and'coals of'fire.

14 The LORD'thundered out of'heaven; *
   the Most'High'uttered his'voice.

15 He loosed his|arrows and|scattered them; *
   he hurled|thunder|bolts and|routed them.

16 The beds of the seas were uncovered,
   and the foundations of the|world laid|bare, *
      at your battle cry, O LORD,
      at the|blast of the|breath of your|nostrils.

17 He reached down from on|high and|grasped me; *
   he drew me|out of|grëat|waters.

18 He delivered me from my strong enemies
   and from|those who|hated me; *
      for|they were too|mighty|for me.

19 They confronted me in the day of|my dis|aster; *
   but the|LORD was|my sup|port.

20 He brought me out into an|open|place; *
   he rescued me be|cause he de|lighted|in me.

Psalm 18: Part 2 *Et retribuet mihi*

36 — *John Goss*

38 — *William Boyce*

21 The LORD rewarded me because of my|righteous|dealing; *
   because my|hands were|clean he re|warded me;

22 For I have kept the|ways of the|LORD *
   and have not of|fended a|gainst my|God;

36

38

William Boyce

23 For all his judgments are be'fore my ' eyes, *
  and his decrees I ' have not ' put a'way from me;

24 For I have been ' blameless with ' him *
  and have ' kept my'self from in'iquity;

†25 Therefore the LORD rewarded me according to my ' righteous ' dealing, *
  because of the cleanness of my ' hands ' in his ' sight.

26 With the faithful you show yourself ' faithful, O ' God; *
  with the forthright you ' show your'sëlf ' forthright.

27 With the pure you ' show yourself ' pure, *
  but with the ' crooked ' you are ' wily.

28 You will save a ' lowly ' people, *
  but you will ' humble the ' haughty ' eyes.

29 You, O ' LORD, are my ' lamp; *
  my God, you ' make my ' darkness ' bright.

30 With you I will break ' down an en'closure; *
  with the help of my God I will ' scäle ' any ' wall.

31 As for God, his ways are perfect;
  the words of the LORD are ' tried in the ' fire; *
  he is a ' shield to ' all who ' trust in him.

32 For who is 'God, but the 'LORD? *
    who is the 'Rock, ex'cept our 'God?

33 It is God who girds me a'bout with 'strength *
    and 'makes my 'way se'cure.

34 He makes me sure'footed like a 'deer *
    and lets me stand 'firm 'on the 'heights.

35 He trains my 'hands for 'battle *
    and my arms for bending 'even a 'bow of 'bronze.

36 You have given me your 'shield of 'victory; *
    your right hand also sustains me;
    your loving 'cäre 'makes me 'great.

37 You lengthen my 'stride be'neath me, *
    and my 'ankles do 'not give 'way.

38 I pursue my enemies and 'over'take them; *
    I will not turn 'back till I 'have de'stroyed them.

39 I strike them down, and they 'cannot 'rise; *
    they fall de'feated 'at my 'feet.

40 You have girded me with 'strength for the 'battle; *
    you have cast down my adversaries beneath me;
    you have 'put my 'enemies to 'flight.

41 I destroy those who hate me;
    they cry out, but there is 'none to 'help them; *
    they cry to the 'LORD, but he 'does not 'answer.

42 I beat them like 'dust before the 'wind; *
    I trample them like 'müd 'in the 'streets.

43 You deliver me from the 'strife of the 'peoples; *
    you put me at the 'hëad 'of the 'nations.

44 A people I have not known shall serve me;
    no sooner shall they hear than 'they shall o'bey me; *
    —'strangers will 'cringe be'fore me.

45 The foreign peoples will 'löse 'heart; *
    they shall come 'trembling 'out of their 'strongholds.

36

John Goss

38

William Boyce

46 The LORD lives! |Blessèd is my|Rock! *
   Exalted is the|God of|my sal|vation!

47 He is the God who|gave me|victory *
   and cast|down the|peoples be|neath me.

48 You rescued me from the fury of my enemies;
   you exalted me above those who|rose a|gainst me; *
   you|saved me from my|deadly|foe.

49 Therefore will I extol you among the|nations, O|LORD, *
   and sing|praises|to your|Name.

†50 He multiplies the|victories of his|king; *
   he shows loving-kindness to his anointed,
   to David and|his des|cendants for|ever.

32

Psalm 19 *Caeli enarrant*

39

Samuel Sebastian Wesley

40

Stephen Darlington

1 The heavens declare the ˈglory of ˈGod, *
    ˎand the ˈfirmament ˈshows his ˈhandiwork.

2 One day tells its ˈtale to anˈother, *
    and one night imparts ˈknowledge ˈto anˈother.

3 Although they have no ˈwords or ˈlanguage, *
    and their ˈvoices ˈare not ˈheard,

4 Their sound has gone out into ˈäll ˈlands, *
    and their message to the ˈeṅds ˈof the ˈworld.

5 In the deep has he set a paˈvilion for the ˈsun; *
    it comes forth like a bridegroom out of his chamber;
    it rejoices like a ˈchampion to ˈrun its ˈcourse.

6 It goes forth from the uttermost edge of the heavens
    and runs about to the ˈend of it aˈgain; *
    nothing is ˈhidden from its ˈburning ˈheat.

7 The law of the LORD is perfect and reˈvives the ˈsoul; *
    the testimony of the LORD is sure and gives ˈwisdom ˈto the ˈinnocent.

8 The statutes of the LORD are just and reˈjoice the ˈheart; *
    the commandment of the LORD is clear and gives ˈlïght ˈto the ˈeyes.

33

39

Samuel Sebastian Wesley

40

Stephen Darlington

9 The fear of the LORD is clean and en'dures for 'ever; *
 the judgments of the LORD are true and 'righteous 'alto'gether.

10 More to be desired are they than gold, more than 'much fine 'gold, *
 sweeter far than honey, than 'honey 'in the 'comb.

11 By them also is your 'servant en'lightened, *
 and in keeping them 'there is 'great re'ward.

12 Who can tell how 'often he of'fends? *
 — 'cleanse me from my 'secret 'faults.

13 Above all, keep your servant from presumptuous sins;
 let them not get do'minion 'over 'me; *
  then shall I be whole and sound,
  and 'innocent of a 'great of'fense.

14 Let the words of my mouth and the meditation of my
   heart be ac'ceptable in your 'sight, *
 O LORD, my 'strength and 'my re'deemer.

Psalm 20   *Exaudiat te Dominus*

41   *Matthew Camidge*

42   *John Robinson*

1 May the LORD answer you in the⸍day of⸍trouble, *
   the Name of the⸍God of⸍Jacob de⸍fend you;

2 Send you help from his⸍holy⸍place *
   and⸍strengthen you⸍out of⸍Zion;

3 Remember⸍all your⸍offerings *
   and ac⸍cept your⸍burnt⸍sacrifice;

4 Grant you your⸍heart's de⸍sire *
   and⸍prosper⸍all your⸍plans.

†5 We will shout for joy at your victory
   and triumph in the⸍Name of our⸍God; *
      may the LORD grant⸍all⸍your re⸍quests.

6 Now I know that the LORD gives victory to⸍his a⸍nointed: *
   he will answer him out of his holy heaven,
      with the victorious⸍strength of⸍his right⸍hand.

7 Some put their trust in chariots and⸍some in⸍horses, *
   but we will call upon the⸍Name of the⸍LORD our⸍God.

8 They collapse and⸍fall⸍down, *
   but we will a⸍rise and⸍stand⸍upright.

9 O LORD, give⸍victory to the⸍king *
   and⸍answer us⸍when we⸍call.

Psalm 21   *Domine, in virtute tua*

43   *Highmore Skeats, Jr.*

44   *Percy Buck*

1 The king rejoices in your ' strength, O ' LORD; *
   how greatly he ex'ülts ' in your ' victory!

2 You have given him his ' heart's de'sire; *
   you have not de'nied him the re'quest of his ' lips.

3 For you meet him with ' blessings of pros'perity, *
   and set a crown of fine ' gold up'on his ' head.

4 He asked you for life, and you ' gave it to ' him: *
   length of ' days, for ' ever and ' ever.

5 His honor is great, be'cause of your ' victory; *
   splendor and majesty have ' you be'stowed up'on him.

6 For you will give him ever'lasting fe'licity *
   and will make him ' glad with the ' joy of your ' presence.

†7 For the king puts his ' trust in the ' LORD; *
   because of the loving-kindness of the Most ' High, he ' will not ' fall.

8 Your hand will lay hold upon ' all your ' enemies; *
   your right hand will ' seize all ' those who ' hate you.

9 You will make them like a ' fiery ' furnace *
   at the ' time of your ap'pearing, O ' LORD;

10 You will swallow them ꞌup in your ꞌwrath, *
    and ꞌfire ꞌshall con ꞌsume them.

11 You will destroy their ꞌoffspring from the ꞌland *
    and their descendants from among the ꞌpeoples ꞌof the ꞌearth.

12 Though they intend evil against you
    and devise ꞌwicked ꞌschemes, *
      yet ꞌthey shall ꞌnot pre ꞌvail.

13 For you will ꞌput them to ꞌflight *
    and ꞌaim your ꞌarrows at ꞌthem.

†14 Be exalted, O ꞌLORD, in your ꞌmight; *
    we will ꞌsing and ꞌpraise your ꞌpower.

Psalm 22 *Deus, Deus meus*

45 *Edward John Hopkins*

47 *Alec Wyton*

Setting 1: #45–46; setting 2: #47–48.

1 My God, my God, why have 'you for'saken me? *
  and are so far from my cry
  and from the 'words of 'my dis'tress?

2 O my God, I cry in the daytime, but you 'do not 'answer; *
  by night as 'well, but I 'find no 'rest.

3 Yet you are the 'Holy 'One, *
  en'throned upon the 'praises of 'Israel.

4 Our forefathers 'put their 'trust in you; *
  they 'trusted, and 'you de'livered them.

5 They cried out to you and 'were de'livered; *
  they trusted in 'you and were 'not put to 'shame.

6 But as for me, I am a 'worm and no 'man, *
  scorned by 'all and des'pised by the 'people.

7 All who see me 'laugh me to 'scorn; *
  they curl their lips and 'wag their 'heäds, 'saying,

8 "He trusted in the LORD; 'let him de'liver him; *
  let him 'rescue him, if 'he de'lights in him."

38

9 Yet you are he who took me'out of the'womb, *
   and kept me'safe upon my'mother's'breast.

10 I have been entrusted to you ever'since I was'born; *
   you were my God when I was'still in my'mother's'womb.

11 Be not far from me, for'trouble is'near, *
   and'there is'none to'help.

12 Many young'bulls en'circle me; *
   strong'bulls of'Bashan sur'round me.

13 They open'wide their'jaws at me, *
   like a'ravening and a'roaring'lion.

14 I am poured out like water;
   all my bones are'out of'joint; *
      my heart within my'breast is'melting'wax.

15 My mouth is dried out like a pot-sherd;
   my tongue sticks to the'roof of my'mouth; *
      and you have'laid me in the'dust of the'grave.

16 Packs of dogs close me in,
   and gangs of evildoers'circle a'round me; *
      they pierce my hands and my feet;
      I can'coünt'all my'bones.

17 They'stare and gloat'over me; *
      they divide my garments among them;
      they cast'löts'for my'clothing.

18 Be not far a'way, O'LORD; *
   you are my'strëngth,'hasten to'help me.

19 Save me'from the'sword, *
   my'life from the'power of the'dog.

20 Save me from the'lion's'mouth, *
   my wretched body from the'horns of'wïld'bulls.

†21 I will declare your'Name to my'brethren; *
   in the midst of the congre'gation'I will'praise you.

Edward John Hopkins

48

Andrew Seivewright

22 Praise the LORD, | you that | fear him; *

    stand in awe of him, O offspring of Israel;

    all you of | Jacob's | line, give | glory.

23 For he does not despise nor abhor the poor in their poverty;

    neither does he | hide his | face from them; *

    but when they | cry to | him he | hears them.

24 My praise is of him in the | great as | sembly; *

    I will perform my vows in the | presence of | those who | worship him.

25 The poor shall eat and be satisfied,

    and those who seek the | LORD shall | praise him: *

    "May your | heärt | live for | ever!"

26 All the ends of the earth shall remember and | turn to the | LORD, *

    and all the families of the | nations shall | bow be | fore him.

27 For kingship be | longs to the | LORD; *

    he | rüles | over the | nations.

28 To him alone all who sleep in the earth bow | down in | worship; *

    all who go down to the | düst | fall be | fore him.

29 My soul shall live for him;

    my des | cendants shall | serve him; *

    they shall be | known as the | LORD's for | ever.

†30 They shall come and make known to a⸆people yet un⸆born *
the saving⸆deeds that⸆he has⸆done.

Psalm 23 *Dominus regit me*

49

John Goss

50

Edward Cuthbert Bairstow

1 The⸆LORD is my⸆shepherd; *
   I⸆shall not⸆be in⸆want.

2 He makes me lie⸆down in green⸆pastures *
   and⸆leads me be⸆side still⸆waters.

3 He re⸆vives my⸆soul *
   and guides me along right⸆pathways for his⸆Näme's⸆sake.

4 Though I walk through the valley of the shadow of death,
   I shall⸆fear no⸆evil; *
      for you are with me;
      your⸆rod and your⸆staff, they⸆comfort me.

5 You spread a table before me in the presence of⸆those who⸆trouble me; *
      you have anointed my head with oil,
      and my⸆cup is⸆running⸆over.

6 Surely your goodness and mercy shall follow me all
            the⸆days of my⸆life, *
      and I will dwell in the⸆house of the⸆LORD for⸆ever.

Psalm 24 *Domini est terra*

51 *George Thalben-Ball*

52 *William Crotch*

1 The earth is the LORD's and 'all that is 'in it, *
    the world and 'all who 'dwell there 'in.

2 For it is he who founded it up 'on the 'seas *
    and made it firm upon the 'rivers 'of the 'deep.

3 "Who can ascend the 'hill of the 'LORD? *
    and who can 'stand in his 'holy 'place?"

4 "Those who have clean hands and a 'püre 'heart, *
    who have not pledged themselves to falsehood,
    nor 'sworn by 'what is a 'fraud.

5 They shall receive a 'blessing from the 'LORD *
    and a just reward from the 'God of 'their sal 'vation."

6 Such is the generation of 'those who 'seek him, *
    of those who seek your 'face, O 'God of 'Jacob.

7 Lift up your heads, O gates;
    lift them high, O ever 'lasting 'doors; *
    and the King of 'glory 'shall come 'in.

8 "Who is this 'King of 'glory?" *
    "The LORD, strong and mighty,
    the 'LÖRD, 'mighty in 'battle."

42

9   Lift up your heads, O gates;
    lift them high, O ever'lasting'doors; *
        and the King of'glory'shall come'in.

10 "Who is he, this'King of'glory?" *
    "The LORD of hosts,
        'he is the'King of'glory."

Psalm 25   *Ad te, Domine, levavi*

53

William Crotch

54

Henry Stonex

1   To you, O LORD, I lift up my soul;
    my God, I put my'trust in'you; *
        let me not be humiliated,
        nor let my'enemies'triumph'over me.

2   Let none who look to you be'put to'shame; *
        let the treacherous be disap'pointed'in their'schemes.

3   Show me your'ways, O'LORD, *
        and'teach'me your'paths.

4   Lead me in your'truth and'teach me, *
        for you are the God of my salvation;
        in you have I trusted'all the'däy'long.

William Crotch

Henry Stonex

5 Remember, O LORD, your com'passion and 'love, *
   for 'they are from 'ever'lasting.

6 Remember not the sins of my youth and 'my trans'gressions; *
   remember me according to your love,
   and for the 'sake of your 'goodness, O 'LORD.

7 Gracious and 'upright is the 'LORD; *
   therefore he teaches 'sinners 'in his 'way.

8 He guides the humble in 'doing 'right *
   and teaches his 'wäy 'to the 'lowly.

9 All the paths of the LORD are 'love and 'faithfulness *
   to those who keep his 'covenant 'and his 'testimonies.

10 For your 'Name's sake, O 'LORD, *
   forgive my 'sin, for 'it is 'great.

11 Who are they who 'fear the 'LORD? *
   he will teach them the 'way that 'they should 'choose.

12 They shall 'dwell in pros'perity, *
   and their 'offspring shall in'herit the 'land.

13 The LORD is a friend to'those who'fear him *
  —'and will'show them his'covenant.

14 My eyes are ever'looking to the'LORD, *
  for he shall pluck my'feet'out of the'net.

15 Turn to me and have'pity on'me, *
  for I am'left a'lone and in'misery.

16 The sorrows of my'heart have in'creased; *
  —'bring me'out of my'troubles.

17 Look upon my ad'versity and'misery *
  and for'give me'all my'sin.

18 Look upon my enemies, for'they are'many, *
  and they bear a'violent'hatred a'gainst me.

19 Protect my'life and de'liver me; *
  let me not be put to shame, for'I have'trusted in'you.

20 Let integrity and'uprightness pre'serve me, *
  for my'hope has'been in'you.

†21 Deliver'Israel, O'God, *
  —'out of'all his'troubles.

Psalm 26
Judica me, Domine

55

Richard Farrant

56

Thomas Attwood Walmisley

1 Give judgment for me, O LORD,
   for I have ⌐lived with in⌐tegrity; *
   I have trusted in the⌐Lord and⌐have not⌐faltered.

2 Test me, O⌐LORD, and⌐try me; *
   ex⌐amine my⌐heart and my⌐mind.

3 For your love is be⌐fore my⌐eyes; *
   I have⌐walked⌐faithfully with⌐you.

4 I have not⌐sat with the⌐worthless, *
   nor do I con⌐sört⌐with the de⌐ceitful.

5 I have hated the company of⌐evil⌐doers; *
   I will⌐not sit⌐down with the⌐wicked.

6 I will wash my hands in⌐innocence, O⌐LORD, *
   that I may go in pro⌐cession⌐round your⌐altar,

7 Singing aloud a⌐song of⌐thanksgiving *
   and recounting⌐all your⌐wonderful⌐deeds.

8 LORD, I love the house in⌐which you⌐dwell *
   and the⌐place where your⌐glory a⌐bides.

9 Do not sweep me a⌐way with⌐sinners, *
   nor my life with⌐those who⌐thirst for⌐blood,

10 Whose hands are full of'evil'plots, *
   and their'right hand'full of'bribes.

11 As for me, I will'live with in'tegrity; *
   redeem me, O'LORD and have'pity on'me.

12 My foot stands on'level'ground; *
   in the full assembly'I will'bless the'LORD.

Psalm 27   *Dominus illuminatio*

57

James Turle

58

Ivor Algernon Atkins

1 The LORD is my light and my salvation;
   whom then'shall I'fear? *
      the LORD is the strength of my life;
      of whom then'shall I'be a'fraid?

2 When evildoers came upon me to eat'up my'flesh, *
   it was they, my foes and my'adversaries, who'stumbled and'fell.

3 Though an army should en'camp a'gainst me, *
   yet my'heart shall not'be a'fraid;

4 And though war should rise'up a'gainst me, *
   yet will I'put my'trust in'him.

57   *James Turle*

58   *Ivor Algernon Atkins*

5 One thing have I asked of the LORD;
  ¦one thing I¦seek; *
    that I may dwell in the house of the¦LORD all the¦days of my¦life;

6 To behold the fair¦beauty of the¦LORD *
    and to¦seek him¦in his¦temple.

7 For in the day of trouble he shall keep me¦safe in his¦shelter; *
    he shall hide me in the secrecy of his dwelling
    and set me¦high up¦on a¦rock.

8 Even now he lifts¦up my¦head *
    above my¦enemies¦round a¦bout me.

†9 Therefore I will offer in his dwelling an oblation
  with¦sounds of great¦gladness; *
    I will sing and make¦music¦to the¦LORD.

10 Hearken to my voice, O¦LORD, when I¦call; *
    have¦mercy on¦me and¦answer me.

11 You speak in my heart and say,¦"Seek my¦face," *
    Your¦face, LORD,¦will I seek.

12 Hide not your ' face ' from me, *
    nor turn away your ' servant ' in dis ' pleasure.

13 You have been my helper;
    cast me ' not a ' way; *
    do not forsake me, O ' God of ' my sal ' vation.

†14 Though my father and my ' mother for ' sake me, *
    the ' LORD ' will sus ' tain me.

15 Show me your ' way, O ' LORD; *
    lead me on a level ' path, be ' cause of my ' enemies.

16 Deliver me not into the ' hand of my ' adversaries, *
    for false witnesses have risen up against me,
    and also ' those who ' speak ' malice.

17 What if I had not believed
    that I should see the ' goodness of the ' LORD *
    in the ' land ' of the ' living!

18 O tarry and await the LORD's pleasure;
    be strong, and he shall ' comfort your ' heart; *
    wait ' patiently ' for the ' LORD.

Psalm 28 *Ad te, Domine*

59 *Sydney Nicholson*

60 *George J. Elvey*

1 O Lord, I call to you;
  my Rock, do not be'deaf to my'cry; *
    lest, if you do not hear me,
    I become like'those who go'down to the'Pit.

2 Hear the voice of my prayer when I cry'out to'you, *
    when I lift up my'hands to your'holy of'holies.

3 Do not snatch me away with the wicked or with the'evil'doers, *
    who speak peaceably with their neighbors,
    while'strife is'in their'hearts.

4 Repay them ac'cording to their'deeds, *
    and according to the'wickedness'of their'actions.

5 According to the work of their'hands re'pay them, *
    and'give them their'just de'serts.

6 They have no understanding of the Lord's doings,
  nor of the'works of his'hands; *
    therefore he will break them'down and not'build them'up.

7 Blessèd'is the'Lord! *
    for he has'heard the'voice of my'prayer.

8 The Lord is my'strength and my'shield; *
    my heart trusts in'him, and'I have been'helped;

50

†9 Therefore my heart 'dances for 'joy, *
　　and in my 'song 'will I 'praise him.

10 The LORD is the 'strength of his 'people, *
　　a safe 'refuge for 'his a'nointed.

11 Save your people and 'bless your in'heritance; *
　　shepherd them and 'carry 'them for 'ever.

Psalm 29 *Afferte Domino*

61

Ray Francis Brown

62

Percy Buck

1 Ascribe to the 'LORD, you 'gods, *
　　ascribe to the 'LORD 'glory and 'strength.

2 Ascribe to the LORD the glory 'due his 'Name; *
　　worship the 'LORD in the 'beauty of 'holiness.

3 The voice of the LORD is upon the waters;
　　the God of 'glory 'thunders; *
　　the LORD is up'on the 'mighty 'waters.

4 The voice of the LORD is a 'powerful 'voice; *
　　the voice of the 'LORD is a 'voice of 'splendor.

61 *Ray Francis Brown*

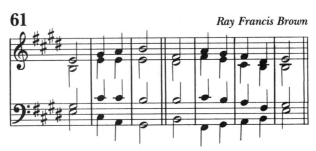

62 *Percy Buck*

5 The voice of the LORD 'breaks the 'cedar trees; *
   the LORD 'breaks the 'cedars of 'Lebanon;

6 He makes Lebanon 'skip like a 'calf, *
   and Mount Hermon 'like a 'young wild 'ox.

7 The voice of the LORD splits the flames of fire;
   the voice of the LORD 'shakes the 'wilderness; *
   the LORD 'shakes the 'wilderness of 'Kadesh.

8 The voice of the LORD makes the 'oak trees 'writhe *
   and 'strips the 'forests 'bare.

†9 And in the 'temple of the 'LORD *
   — 'all are 'crying, '"Glory!"

10 The LORD sits enthroned a 'bove the 'flood; *
   the LORD sits enthroned as 'King for 'ever 'more.

11 The LORD shall give 'strength to his 'people; *
   the LORD shall give his 'people the 'blessing of 'peace.

Psalm 30 *Exaltabo te, Domine*

Ray Francis Brown

Gerald Knight

1 I will exalt you, O LORD,
      because you have ˈlifted me ˈup *
            and have not let my ˈenemies ˈtriumph ˈover me.

2 O LORD my God, I cried ˈout to ˈyou, *
      and ˈyou re ˈstored me to ˈhealth.

3 You brought me up, O ˈLORD, from the ˈdead; *
      you restored my life as I was ˈgoing ˈdown to the ˈgrave.

4 Sing to the LORD, you ˈservants of ˈhis; *
      give thanks for the re ˈmembrance ˈof his ˈholiness.

5 For his wrath endures but the ˈtwinkling of an ˈeye, *
      his ˈfavor ˈfor a ˈlifetime.

6 Weeping may ˈspend the ˈnight, *
      but ˈjöy ˈcomes in the ˈmorning.

7 While I felt secure, I said,
      "I shall ˈnever be dis ˈturbed. *
            You, LORD, with your favor, made me as ˈströng ˈas the ˈmountains."

8 Then you ˈhid your ˈface, *
      and ˈI was ˈfilled with ˈfear.

53

63

Ray Francis Brown

64

Gerald Knight

9 I cried to ˈyou, O ˈLORD; *
 Iˈpleaded with the ˈLÖRD, ˈsaying,

10 "What profit is there in my blood, if I goˈdown to theˈPit? *
 will the dustˈpraise you or deˈclare yourˈfaithfulness?

11 Hear, O LORD, and haveˈmercy upˈon me; *
 OˈLÖRD, ˈbe myˈhelper."

12 You have turned myˈwailing intoˈdancing; *
 you have put off myˈsack-cloth andˈclothed me withˈjoy.

†13 Therefore my heart sings toˈyou withoutˈceasing; *
 O LORD my God, I willˈgive youˈthanks forˈever.

54

Psalm 31 *In te, Domine, speravi*

65 *James Turle*

66 *Joseph Barnby*

1 In you, O LORD, have I taken refuge;
let me never be ᵓput to ᵓshame; *
de'liver me ᵓin your ᵓrighteousness.

2 In'cline your ᵓear to me; *
make ᵓhäste ᵓto de'liver me.

3 Be my strong rock, a castle to keep me safe,
for you are my ᵓcrag and my ᵓstronghold; *
for the sake of your ᵓNäme, ᵓlead me and ᵓguide me.

4 Take me out of the net that they have ᵓsecretly ᵓset for me, *
for ᵓyou are my ᵓtower of ᵓstrength.

†5 Into your hands I com'mend my ᵓspirit, *
for you have redeemed me,
O ᵓLORD, O ᵓGod of ᵓtruth.

6 I hate those who cling to ᵓworthless ᵓidols, *
and I'put my ᵓtrust in the ᵓLORD.

7 I will rejoice and be glad be'cause of your ᵓmercy; *
for you have seen my affliction;
you ᵓknöw ᵓmy dis'tress.

55

65

James Turle

66

Joseph Barnby

8 You have not shut me up in the ⹀power of the ⹀enemy; *
   you have set my ⹀feet in an ⹀open ⹀place.

9 Have mercy on me, O LORD, for ⹀I am in ⹀trouble; *
   my eye is consumed with sorrow,
   and ⹀also my ⹀throat and my ⹀belly.

10 For my life is wasted with grief,
   and my ⹀years with ⹀sighing; *
   my strength fails me because of affliction,
   and my ⹀bones ⹀are con⹀sumed.

11 I have become a reproach to all my enemies and even to my neighbors,
   a dismay to those of ⹀my ac⹀quaintance; *
   when they see me in the ⹀street ⹀they a⹀void me.

12 I am forgotten like a dead man, ⹀out of ⹀mind; *
   I am as ⹀useless as a ⹀broken ⹀pot.

13 For I have heard the whispering of the crowd;
   fear is ⹀all a⹀round; *
   they put their head together against me;
   They ⹀plot to ⹀take my ⹀life.

14 But as for me, I have trusted in'you, O'LORD. *
    I have said,'"Yŏu'are my'God.

15 My times are'in your'hand; *
    rescue me from the hand of my enemies,
    and from'those who'persecute'me.

16 Make your face to'shine upon your'servant, *
    and in your'loving'kindness'save me."

17 LORD, let me not be ashamed for having'called upon'you; *
    rather, let the wicked be put to shame;
    let them be'silent'in the'grave.

18 Let the lying lips be silenced which speak a'gainst the'righteous, *
    haughtily, dis'dainfully, and'with con'tempt.

19 How great is your goodness, O LORD!
    which you have laid up for'those who'fear you; *
    which you have done in the sight of all
    for those who'put their'trust in'you.

20 You hide them in the covert of your presence from'those who
                  'slander them; *
    you keep them in your'shelter from the'strife of'tongues.

21 Blessèd'be the'LORD! *
    for he has shown me the wonders of his'love in a be'sieged'city.

†22 Yet I said in my alarm,
    "I have been cut off from the'sight of your'eyes." *
    Nevertheless, you heard the sound of my en'treaty when
                'I cried'out to you.

23 Love the LORD, all'you who'worship him; *
    the LORD protects the faithful,
    but repays to the full'those who'act'haughtily.

24 Be strong and let your'heart take'courage, *
    all'you who'wait for the'LORD.

Psalm 32   *Beati quorum*

67   *James Nares*

68   *Samuel Wesley*

1 Happy are they whose trans'gressions are for'given, *
    and whose 'sin is 'put a'way!

2 Happy are they to whom the LORD im'putes no 'guilt, *
    and in whose 'spirit there 'is no 'guile!

3 While I held my tongue, my bones 'withered a'way, *
    because of my 'groaning 'all day 'long.

4 For your hand was heavy upon me 'day and 'night; *
    my moisture was dried 'up as in the 'heat of 'summer.

5 Then I ack'nowledged my 'sin to you, *
    and 'did not con'ceal my 'guilt.

6 I said, "I will confess my trans'gressions to the 'LORD." *
    Then you forgave me the 'güilt 'of my 'sin.

7 Therefore all the faithful will make their prayers to
                    you in 'time of 'trouble; *
    when the great waters over'flow, they 'shall not 'reach them.

8 You are my hiding-place;
        you pre'serve me from 'trouble; *
        you sur'round me with 'shouts of de'liverance.

58

9 "I will instruct you and teach you in the way that ' you should ' go; *
   I will ' guide you ' with my ' eye.

10 Do not be like horse or mule, which have ' no under ' standing; *
   who must be fitted with bit and bridle,
   or ' else they will ' not stay ' near you."

11 Great are the tribu ' lations of the ' wicked; *
   but mercy embraces ' those who ' trust in the ' LORD.

12 Be glad, you righteous, and re ' joice in the ' LORD; *
   shout for joy, ' all who are ' true of ' heart.

Psalm 33   *Exultate, justi*

69 — *John Randall*

70 — *Richard Woodward, Jr.*

1 Rejoice in the ' LORD, you ' righteous; *
   it is good for the ' just to ' sing ' praises.

2 Praise the ' LORD with the ' harp; *
   play to him upon the ' psalter ' y and ' lyre.

3 Sing for him a ' new ' song; *
   sound a fanfare with all your ' skill up ' on the ' trumpet.

4 For the word of the ' LORD is ' right, *
   and ' all his ' works are ' sure.

69 *John Randall*

70 *Richard Woodward, Jr.*

5 He loves ⌒righteousness and ⌐justice; *
   the loving-kindness of the LORD ⌐fills the ⌐whöle ⌐earth.

6 By the word of the LORD were the ⌐heavens ⌐made, *
   by the breath of his mouth ⌐all the ⌒heavenly ⌐hosts.

7 He gathers up the waters of the ocean as ⌐in a ⌐water-skin *
   and stores up the ⌐deῗths ⌐of the ⌐sea.

8 Let all the earth ⌐fear the ⌐LORD; *
   let all who dwell in the ⌐wörld ⌐stand in ⌐awe of him.

9 For he spoke, and it ⌐came to ⌐pass; *
   he com ⌒manded, and ⌒it ⌐stöod ⌐fast.

10 The LORD brings the will of the ⌒nations to ⌐naught; *
   he thwarts the de ⌐siǧns ⌐of the ⌐peoples.

†11 But the LORD's will stands ⌐fast for ⌐ever, *
   and the designs of his ⌐heart from ⌐age to ⌐age.

12 Happy is the nation whose ⌒God is the ⌐LORD! *
   happy the people he has ⌒chosen to ⌐be his ⌐own!

13 The LORD looks ⌐down from ⌐heaven, *
   and beholds all the ⌐people ⌐in the ⌐world.

14 From where he sits enthroned he'turns his'gaze *
  on'all who'dwell on the'earth.

15 He fashions'all the'hearts of them *
  and under'stands'all their'works.

16 There is no king that can be saved by a'mighty'army; *
  a strong man is not de'livered by'his great'strength.

17 The horse is a vain'hope for de'liverance; *
  for all its'strength it'cannot'save.

18 Behold, the eye of the LORD is upon'those who'fear him, *
  on those who'wait up'on his'love,

19 To pluck their'lives from'death, *
  and to'feed them in'time of'famine.

20 Our soul'waits for the'LORD; *
  he is our'help'and our'shield.

21 Indeed, our heart re'joices in'him, *
  for in his holy'Name we'put our'trust.

†22 Let your loving-kindness, O'LORD, be up'on us, *
  as we have'put our'trust in'you.

Psalm 34 *Benedicam Dominum*

71 *Thomas Norris*

72 *J. Marcus Ritchie*

1 I will bless the 'LORD at 'all times; *
  his praise shall 'ever be 'in my 'mouth.

2 I will 'glory in the 'LORD; *
  let the 'humble 'hear and re'joice.

3 Proclaim with me the 'greatness of the 'LORD; *
  let us ex'alt his 'Name to'gether.

4 I sought the 'LORD, and he 'answered me *
  and delivered me 'out of 'all my 'terror.

5 Look upon 'him and be 'radiant, *
  and let not your 'faces 'be a'shamed.

6 I called in my affliction and the 'LÖRD 'heard me *
  and 'saved me from 'all my 'troubles.

7 The angel of the LORD encompasses 'those who 'fear him, *
  and 'hë 'will de'liver them.

8 Taste and see that the 'LORD is 'good; *
  — 'happy are 'they who 'trust in him!

9 Fear the LORD, you that 'are his 'saints, *
  for 'those who 'fear him lack 'nothing.

10 The young lions lack and ꞌsufferꞌhunger, *

    but those who seek the LORD lackꞌnothingꞌthat isꞌgood.

11 Come, children, andꞌlisten toꞌme; *

    I willꞌteach you theꞌfear of theꞌLORD.

12 Who amongꞌyou lovesꞌlife *

    and desires longꞌlife to enꞌjoy prosꞌperity?

13 Keep your tongue fromꞌevilꞌspeaking *

    and yourꞌlips fromꞌlyingꞌwords.

14 Turn from evil andꞌdöꞌgood; *

    seekꞌpeäceꞌand purꞌsue it.

15 The eyes of the LORD are upꞌon theꞌrighteous, *

    and his ears areꞌopenꞌto theirꞌcry.

16 The face of the LORD is againstꞌthose who doꞌevil, *

    to root out the reꞌmembrance ofꞌthem from theꞌearth.

17 The righteous cry, and theꞌLÖRDꞌhears them *

    and deꞌlivers them fromꞌall theirꞌtroubles.

18 The LORD is near to theꞌbrokenꞌhearted *

    and will saveꞌthose whoseꞌspirits areꞌcrushed.

19 Many are theꞌtroubles of theꞌrighteous, *

    but the LORD will deꞌliver himꞌout of themꞌall.

20 He will keep safeꞌall hisꞌbones; *

    notꞌone ofꞌthem shall beꞌbroken.

21 Evil shallꞌslay theꞌwicked, *

    and those who hate theꞌrighteousꞌwill beꞌpunished.

22 The LORD ransoms theꞌlife of hisꞌservants, *

    andꞌnone will beꞌpunished whoꞌtrust in him.

Psalm 35   *Judica, Domine*

73   *William Crotch*

74   *Thomas Attwood*

1 Fight those who ⏜fight me, O ˈLORD; *
    attack ˈthose who are atˈtacking ˈme.

2 Take up ˈshield and ˈarmor *
    and ˈrise ˈup to ˈhelp me.

3 Draw the sword and bar the way against ˈthose who purˈsue me; *
    say to my soul, ˈ"I am ˈyour salˈvation."

4 Let those who seek after my life be ˈshamed and ˈhumbled; *
    let those who plot my ruin fall ˈback and ˈbe disˈmayed.

5 Let them be like ˈchaff before the ˈwind, *
    and let the angel of the ˈLORD ˈdrive them aˈway.

6 Let their way be ˈdark and ˈslippery, *
    and let the ˈangel of the ˈLORD purˈsue them.

7 For they have secretly spread a net for me withˈout a ˈcause; *
    without a cause they have dug a ˈpit to ˈtake me aˈlive.

8 Let ruin come upon them ˈunaˈwares; *
    let them be caught in the net they hid;
    let them ˈfall into the ˈpit they ˈdug.

9 Then I will be|joyful in the|LORD; *
  I will|glory|in his|victory.

10 My very bones will say, "LORD,|who is like|you? *
  You deliver the poor from those who are too strong for them,
  the poor and|needy from|those who|rob them."

11 Malicious witnesses rise|up a|gainst me; *
  they charge me with matters|I know|nothing a|bout.

12 They pay me evil in ex|change for|good; *
  my|soul is|full of des|pair.

13 But when they were sick I|dressed in|sack-cloth *
  and|humbled my|self by|fasting;

14 I prayed with my whole heart,
  as one would for a|friend or a|brother; *
  I behaved like one who mourns for his mother,
  |bowed|down and|grieving.

15 But when I stumbled, they were glad and gathered together;
  they|gathered a|gainst me; *
  strangers whom I did not know tore me to|pieces and|would not|stop.

16 They put me to the|test and|mocked me; *
  they|gnashed at me|with their|teeth.

17 O Lord, how long will you|look|on? *
  rescue me from the roaring beasts,
  and my|life from the|young|lions.

18 I will give you thanks in the|great congre|gation; *
  I will|praise you in the|mighty|throng.

19 Do not let my treacherous foes re|joice|over me, *
  nor let those who hate me without a|cause|wink at each|other.

20 For they do not|plan for|peace, *
  but invent deceitful schemes against the|quiet|in the|land.

73

William Crotch

74

Thomas Attwood

21 They opened their mouths at | me and | said, *
  "Aha! we | saw it with our | own | eyes."

22 You saw it, O LORD; | do not be | silent; *
  O | LÖRD, | be not | far from me.

23 Awake, a | rise to my | cause! *
  to my de | fense, my | God and my | Lord!

24 Give me justice, O LORD my God,
  ac | cording to your | righteousness; *
  do not | let them | triumph | over me.

25 Do not let them say in their hearts,
  "Aha! | just what we | want!" *
  Do not let them say, | "We have | swallowed him | up."

26 Let all who rejoice at my ruin be a | shamed and dis | graced; *
  let those who boast against me be | clothed with dis | may and | shame.

27 Let those who favor my cause sing out with | joy and be | glad; *
  let them say always, "Great is the LORD,
  who desires the pros | perity | of his | servant."

28 And my tongue shall be | talking of your | righteousness *
  and of your | präise | all the day | long.

Psalm 36   *Dixit injustus*

75   *John Blow*

77   *John Goss*

Setting 1: #75–76; setting 2: #77–78.

1 There is a voice of rebellion deep in the ˈheart of the ˈwicked; *
   there is no fear of ˈGod be ˈfore his ˈeyes.

2 He flatters himself in his ˈown ˈeyes *
   that his hateful ˈsin will ˈnot be found ˈout.

3 The words of his mouth are ˈwicked and de ˈceitful; *
   he has left off acting ˈwisely and ˈdoing ˈgood.

4 He thinks up wickedness upon his bed
   and has set himself in ˈno good ˈway; *
   he does not ab ˈhör ˈthat which is ˈevil.

   Tune change

67

76

John Stainer

78

John Goss

5 Your love, O LORD, ˈreaches to theˈheavens, *
    and yourˈfaithfulnessˈto theˈclouds.

6 Your righteousness is like the strong mountains,
    your justice like theˈgrëatˈdeep; *
    you save bothˈman andˈbeast, OˈLORD.

7 How priceless is yourˈlove, OˈGod! *
    your people take refuge under theˈshadowˈof your wings.

8 They feast upon the aˈbundance of yourˈhouse; *
    you give them drink from theˈriver ofˈyour deˈlights.

9 For with you is theˈwell ofˈlife, *
    and in yourˈlïghtˈwe seeˈlight.

10 Continue your loving-kindness toˈthose whoˈknow you, *
    and your favor toˈthose who areˈtrue ofˈheart.

11 Let not the foot of theˈproud comeˈnear me, *
    nor the hand of theˈwickedˈpush me aˈside.

12 See how they are fallen, ˈthose who workˈwickedness! *
    they are cast down and shallˈnot beˈable toˈrise.

Psalm 37: Part I   *Noli aemulari*

79

John Goss (after Jeremiah Clarke)

81

John Joubert

Setting 1: #79–80; setting 2: #81.

1 Do not fret yourself because of ˈevilˈdoers; *
  do not be ˈjealous of ˈthose who do ˈwrong.

2 For they shall soon ˈwither like the ˈgrass, *
  and like the green ˈgräss ˈfade a ˈway.

3 Put your trust in the ˈLORD and do ˈgood; *
  dwell in the ˈland and ˈfeed on its ˈriches.

4 Take de ˈlight in the ˈLORD, *
  and he shall ˈgive you your ˈheart's de ˈsire.

5 Commit your way to the LORD and ˈput your ˈtrust in him, *
  and ˈhe will ˈbring it to ˈpass.

6 He will make your righteousness as ˈclear as the ˈlight *
  and your just ˈdealing ˈas the ˈnoonday.

7 Be still be ˈfore the ˈLORD *
  and ˈwäit ˈpatiently ˈfor him.

8 Do not fret yourself over the ˈone who ˈprospers, *
  the one who suc ˈceeds in ˈevil ˈschemes.

79

81

John Joubert

9 Refrain from anger, leave ˈrage aˈlone; *
  do not fret yourself; it ˈleäds ˈonly to ˈevil.

10 For evildoers shall be ˈcüt ˈoff, *
  but those who wait upon the ˈLORD shall posˈsess the ˈland.

11 In a little while the wicked shall be ˈnö ˈmore; *
  you shall search out their place, but ˈthey will ˈnot be ˈthere.

12 But the lowly shall posˈsess the ˈland; *
  they will deˈlight in aˈbundance of ˈpeace.

13 The wicked plot aˈgainst the ˈrighteous *
  and ˈgnash at them ˈwith their ˈteeth.

14 The LORD ˈlaughs at the ˈwicked, *
  because he ˈsees that their ˈday will ˈcome.

15 The wicked draw their sword and bend their bow
  to strike down the ˈpoor and ˈneedy, *
  to slaughter those who are ˈupright ˈin their ˈways.

16 Their sword shall go through their ˈoẅn ˈheart, *
  and their ˈböw ˈshall be ˈbroken.

17 The little that the ˈrighteous ˈhas *
  is better than great ˈriches ˈof the ˈwicked.

18 For the power of the ˈwicked shall be ˈbroken, *
  but the ˈLORD upˈholds the ˈrighteous.

Psalm 37: Part II   *Novit Dominus*

80   *John Goss*

81   *John Joubert*

19 The LORD cares for the ⌐lives of the ⌐godly, *
    and their in⌐heritance shall ⌐last for ⌐ever.

20 They shall not be ashamed in ⌐bäd ⌐times, *
    and in days of famine ⌐they shall ⌐have e⌐nough.

†21 As for the wicked, ⌐they shall ⌐perish, *
    and the enemies of the LORD, like the
                glory of the meadows, shall vanish;
    ⌐they shall ⌐vanish like ⌐smoke.

22 The wicked borrow and do ⌐not re⌐pay, *
    but the ⌐righteous are ⌐generous in ⌐giving.

23 Those who are blessed by God shall pos⌐sess the ⌐land, *
    but those who are ⌐cursed by him shall ⌐be des⌐troyed.

24 Our steps are di⌐rected by the ⌐LORD; *
    he strengthens ⌐those in whose ⌐way he de⌐lights.

25 If they stumble, they shall ⌐not fall ⌐headlong, *
    for the LORD ⌐holds them ⌐by the ⌐hand.

†26 I have been young and ⌐now I am ⌐old, *
    but never have I seen the righteous forsaken,
    or their ⌐children ⌐begging ⌐bread.

71

80

81

27 The righteous are always generous ꞌin their ꞌlending, *
   and their ꞌchildren shall ꞌbe a ꞌblessing.

28 Turn from evil, and ꞌdö ꞌgood, *
   and ꞌdwell in the ꞌland for ꞌever.

29 For the ꞌLORD loves ꞌjustice; *
   he ꞌdoes not for ꞌsake his ꞌfaithful ones.

30 They shall be kept ꞌsafe for ꞌever, *
   but the offspring of the ꞌwicked shall ꞌbe des ꞌtroyed.

31 The righteous shall pos ꞌsess the ꞌland *
   and ꞌdwell in ꞌit for ꞌever.

32 The mouth of the righteous ꞌutters ꞌwisdom, *
   and their ꞌtoṅgue ꞌspeaks what is ꞌright.

33 The law of their God is ꞌin their ꞌheart, *
   and their ꞌfootsteps ꞌshall not ꞌfalter.

34 The wicked ꞌspy on the ꞌrighteous *
   and ꞌseek oc ꞌcasion to ꞌkill them.

35 The LORD will not abandon them ꞌto their ꞌhand, *
   nor let them be found ꞌguilty when ꞌbrought to ꞌtrial.

36 Wait upon the LORD and'keep his'way; *

he will raise you up to possess the land,
and when the wicked are cut'öff,'you will'see it.

37 I have seen the'wicked in their'arrogance, *

flourishing'like a'tree in full'leaf.

38 I went by, and behold,'they were not'there; *

I searched for them, but'they could'not be'found.

39 Mark those who are honest;

ob'serve the'upright; *
for there is a'future'for the'peaceable.

40 Transgressors shall be destroyed,'one and'all; *

the future of the'wicked is'cüt'off.

41 But the deliverance of the righteous'comes from the'LORD; *

he is their'stronghold in'time of'trouble.

42 The LORD will'help them and'rescue them; *

he will rescue them from the wicked and deliver them,
be'cause they seek'refuge in'him.

73

Psalm 38   *Domine, ne in furore*

82   *John Fenstermaker*

83   *Charles Villiers Stanford*

1 O LORD, do not rebuke me ˈin your ˈanger; *
     do not ˈpunish me ˈin your ˈwrath.

2 For your arrows have alˈready ˈpierced me, *
     and your hand ˈpresses ˈhard upˈon me.

3 There is no health in my flesh,
     because of your ˈindigˈnation; *
     there is no soundness in my ˈbody, beˈcause of my ˈsin.

4 For my iniquities ˈoverˈwhelm me; *
     like a heavy burden they are too ˈmuch for ˈme to ˈbear.

5 My wounds ˈstink and ˈfester *
     by ˈreason ˈof my ˈfoolishness.

6 I am utterly bowed ˈdown and ˈprostrate; *
     I go about in ˈmourning ˈall the day ˈlong.

7 My loins are filled with ˈsearing ˈpain; *
     there is no ˈhëalth ˈin my ˈbody.

8 I am utterly ˈnumb and ˈcrushed; *
     I wail, because of the ˈgroaning ˈof my ˈheart.

9 O LORD, you know 'all my de'sires, *
    and my sighing 'is not 'hidden from 'you.

10 My heart is pounding, my 'strength has 'failed me; *
    and the 'brightness of my 'eyes is 'gone from me.

11 My friends and companions draw back from 'my af'fliction; *
    my 'neighbors 'stand afar 'off.

12 Those who seek after my 'life lay 'snares for me; *
    those who strive to hurt me speak of my ruin
    and plot 'treachery 'all the day 'long.

13 But I am like the deaf who 'do not 'hear, *
    like those who are mute and 'do not 'open their 'mouth.

14 I have become like one who 'does not 'hear *
    and from whose 'mouth comes 'no de'fense.

15 For in you, O LORD, have I 'fixed my 'hope; *
    you will 'answer me, O 'Lord my 'God.

16 For I said, "Do not let them rejoice at 'my ex'pense, *
    those who gloat over me 'when my 'föot 'slips."

17 Truly, I am on the 'verge of 'falling, *
    and my 'pain is 'always 'with me.

18 I will con'fess my in'iquity *
    and be 'sorry 'for my 'sin.

19 Those who are my enemies without 'cause are 'mighty, *
    and many in number are 'those who 'wrongfully 'hate me.

20 Those who repay evil for 'göod 'slander me, *
    because I follow the 'coürse 'that is 'right.

21 O LORD, 'do not for'sake me; *
    be not 'far from me, 'O my 'God.

22 Make 'haste to 'help me, *
    O 'Lord of 'my sal'vation.

Psalm 39   *Dixi, Custodiam*

84   *Richard Clark*

85   *C. Hylton Stewart*

1 I said, "I will keep watch up'on my'ways, *
    so that I do'not of'fend with my'tongue.

2 I will put a'muzzle on my'mouth *
    while the'wicked are'in my'presence."

3 So I held my tongue and'säid'nothing; *
    I refrained from rash words;
    but my'pain be'came un'bearable.

4 My heart was hot within me;
    while I pondered, the fire'burst into'flame; *
    I'spoke out'with my'tongue:

5 LORD, let me know my end and the'number of my'days, *
    so that I may'know how'short my'life is.

6 You have given me a mere handful of days,
    and my lifetime is as'nothing in your'sight; *
    truly, even those who stand erect are'but a'puff of'wind.

7 We walk about like a shadow,
    and in vain we'are in'turmoil; *
    we heap up riches and'cannot tell'who will'gather them.

8 And now,'what is my'hope? *
    O Lord, my'höpe'is in'you.

76

9 Deliver me from ˈall my transˈgressions *
    and do not ˈmake me the ˈtaunt of the ˈfool.

10 I fell silent and did not ˈopen my ˈmouth, *
    for ˈsurely it was ˈyou that ˈdid it.

11 Take your afˈfliction from ˈme; *
    I am worn down by the ˈblöws ˈof your ˈhand.

12 With rebukes for sin you punish us;
    like a moth you eat away ˈall that is ˈdear to us; *
    truly, everyone is ˈbut a ˈpuff of ˈwind.

13 Hear my prayer, O LORD,
    and give ˈear to my ˈcry; *
    hold not your ˈpeäce ˈat my ˈtears.

14 For I am but a ˈsojourner with ˈyou, *
    a wayfarer, as ˈall my ˈforebears ˈwere.

†15 Turn your gaze from me, that I may be ˈglad aˈgain, *
    before I go my ˈway and ˈam no ˈmore.

Psalm 40   *Expectans, expectavi*

86   *Shirley Hill (after Nicholson)*

87   *Daniel Pinkham*

1 I waited patiently up|on the|LORD; *
   he stooped to|me and|heard my|cry.

2 He lifted me out of the desolate pit, out of the|mire and|clay; *
   he set my feet upon a high cliff and|made my|footing|sure.

3 He put a new song in my mouth,
   a song of|praise to our|God; *
   many shall see, and stand in awe,
   and|put their|trust in the|LORD.

4 Happy are they who|trust in the|LORD! *
   they do not resort to evil spirits or|turn to|false|gods.

5 Great things are they that you have done, O LORD my God!
   how great your|wonders and your|plans for us! *
   there is none who can|be com|pared with|you.

6 Oh, that I could make them|known and|tell them! *
   but they are|more than|I can|count.

7 In a sacrifice and offering you|take no|pleasure *
   (you have|given me|ears to|hear you);

8 Burnt-offering and sin-offering you have 'not re'quired, *
  and so I 'said, "Be'hold, I 'come.

9 In the roll of the book it is 'written con'cerning me: *
  'I love to do your will, O my God;
  your 'law is 'deep in my 'heart.'"

10 I proclaimed righteousness in the 'great congre'gation; *
  behold, I did not restrain my lips;
  and 'that, O 'LORD, you 'know.

11 Your righteousness have I not hidden in my heart;
  I have spoken of your faithfulness and 'your de'liverance; *
  I have not concealed your love and faithfulness from
  the 'grëat 'congre'gation.

12 You are the LORD;
  do not withhold your com'passion from 'me; *
  let your love and your faithfulness 'keep me 'safe for 'ever,

13 For innumerable troubles have crowded upon me;
  my sins have overtaken me, and I 'cannot 'see; *
  they are more in number than the hairs of my head,
  'and my 'heärt 'fails me.

14 Be pleased, O 'LORD, to de'liver me; *
  O 'LORD, make 'haste to 'help me.

15 Let them be ashamed and altogether dismayed
  who seek after my 'life to de'stroy it; *
  let them draw back and be disgraced
  who take 'pleasure in 'my mis'fortune.

16 Let those who say "Aha!" and gloat over me 'be con'founded, *
  be'cause they 'are a'shamed.

17 Let all who seek you rejoice in 'you and be 'glad; *
  let those who love your salvation continually say,
  '"Grëat 'is the 'LORD!"

18 Though I am 'poor and af'flicted, *
  the 'Lord will 'have re'gard for me.

†19 You are my helper and 'my de'liverer; *
  do not 'tarry, 'O my 'God.

Beatus qui intelligit

88

C. Hylton Stewart

89

George Thalben-Ball

1 Happy are they who consider the ˈpoor and ˈneedy! *
   the LORD will deˈliver them in the ˈtime of ˈtrouble.

2 The LORD preserves them and keeps them alive,
   so that they may be ˈhappy in the ˈland; *
     he does not hand them over to the ˈwill ˈof their ˈenemies.

3 The LORD sustains them ˈon their ˈsickbed *
   and ˈministers to ˈthem in their ˈillness.

4 I said, "LORD, be ˈmerciful to ˈme; *
   heal me, for ˈI have ˈsinned aˈgainst you."

5 My enemies are saying wicked ˈthings aˈbout me: *
   "When will he ˈdie, and his ˈnäme ˈperish?"

6 Even if they come to see me, they speak ˈempty ˈwords; *
   their heart collects false rumors;
   they ˈgo outˈside and ˈspread them.

7 All my enemies whisper toˈgether aˈbout me *
   and deˈvïse ˈevil aˈgainst me.

8 "A deadly thing," they say, "has ˈfastened on ˈhim; *
   he has taken to his bed and will ˈnever get ˈup aˈgain."

9 Even my best friend, whom I trusted,
who'bröke'bread with me, *

    has lifted up his'heel and'turned a'gainst me.

10 But you, O LORD, be merciful to me and'raise me'up, *

    and'Ï'shall re'pay them.

11 By this I'know you are'pleased with me, *

    that my enemy'does not'triumph'over me.

12 In my integrity you'hold me'fast, *

    and shall set me be'fore your'face for'ever.

†13 Blessèd be the LORD'God of'Israel, *

    from age to'age. A'men. A'men.

Psalm 42   *Quemadmodum*

90

William Crotch

91

John Fenstermaker

1 As the deer ˈlongs for the ˈwater-brooks, *
   so longs my ˈsoul for ˈyou, O ˈGod.

2 My soul is athirst for God, athirst for the ˈliving ˈGod; *
   when shall I come to apˈpear before the ˈpresence of ˈGod?

3 My tears have been my food ˈday and ˈnight, *
   while all day long they say to me,
   ˈ"Where now ˈis your ˈGod?"

4 I pour out my soul when Iˈthink on these ˈthings: *
   how I went with the multitude and led them ˈinto the ˈhouse of ˈGod,

†5 With the voice of ˈpraise and ˈthanksgiving, *
   among ˈthose who ˈkëep ˈholy-day.

6 Why are you so full of heaviness, ˈO my ˈsoul? *
   and why are you ˈso disˈquieted withˈin me?

7 Put your ˈtrust in ˈGod; *
   for I will yet give thanks to him,
   who is the help of my ˈcountenance, ˈand my ˈGod.

8 My soul is ˈheavy withˈin me; *
   therefore I will remember you from the land of Jordan,
   and from the peak of Mizar aˈmong the ˈheights of ˈHermon.

9 One deep calls to another in the 'noise of your 'cataracts; *
     all your rapids and 'floods have 'göne 'over me.

10 The LORD grants his loving 'kindness in the 'daytime; *
     in the night season his song is with me,
     a 'prayer to the 'God of my 'life.

11 I will say to the God of my strength,
     ' "Why have you for 'gotten me? *
     and why do I go so heavily 'while the 'enemy op 'presses me?

12 While my 'bones are being 'broken, *
     my enemies 'mock me 'to my 'face;

13 All day 'long they 'mock me *
     and say to me, ' "Where now 'is your 'God?"

14 Why are you so full of heaviness, 'O my 'soul? *
     and why are you 'so dis 'quieted with 'in me?

15 Put your 'trust in 'God; *
     for I will yet give thanks to him,
     who is the help of my 'countenance, 'and my 'God.

Psalm 43   *Judica me, Deus*

92   *William Crotch*

93   *John Fenstermaker*

1 Give judgment for me, O God,
    and defend my cause against an un'godly'people; *
        deliver me from the de'ceitful'and the'wicked.

2 For you are the God of my strength;
    why have you'put me from'you? *
        and why do I go so heavily'while the'enemy op'presses me?

3 Send out your light and your truth, that'they may'lead me, *
        and bring me to your holy'hill and'to your'dwelling;

4 That I may go to the altar of God,
    to the God of my'joy and'gladness; *
        and on the harp I will give thanks to'you, O'God my'God.

5 Why are you so full of heaviness,'O my'soul? *
        and why are you'so dis'quieted with'in me?

6 Put your'trust in'God; *
        for I will yet give thanks to him,
            who is the help of my'countenance,'and my'God.

Psalm 44 *Deus, auribus*

94

John Goss

95

David Hurd

1 We have heard with our ears, O God,
our ˈforefathers haveˈtold us, *
    the deeds you did in their days,
    ˈin theˈdays ofˈold.

2 How with your hand you drove the peoples out
and planted ourˈforefathers in theˈland; *
    how you destroyed nations andˈmade yourˈpeopleˈflourish.

3 For they did not take the land by their sword,
nor did their arm win theˈvictoryˈfor them; *
    but your right hand, your arm, and the light of yourˈcountenance,
    beˈcause youˈfavored them.

4 You are myˈKing and myˈGod; *
    you comˈmändˈvictories forˈJacob.

5 Through you we pushedˈback ourˈadversaries; *
    through your Name we trampled onˈthose who roseˈup aˈgainst us.

6 For I do not reˈly onˈmyˈbow, *
    and my swordˈdoes notˈgive me theˈvictory.

94

95

7 Surely, you gave us victory ˈover our ˈadversaries *
    and put ˈthose who ˈhate us to ˈshame.

8 Every day we ˈgloried in ˈGod, *
    and we will ˈpraise your ˈName for ˈever.

9 Nevertheless, you have re ˈjected and ˈhumbled us *
    and do ˈnot go ˈforth with our ˈarmies.

10 You have made us fall back be ˈfore our ˈadversary, *
    — ˈand our ˈenemies have ˈplundered us.

11 You have made us like ˈsheep to be ˈeaten *
    and have ˈscattered us a ˈmong the ˈnations.

12 You are selling your ˈpeople for a ˈtrifle *
    and are making no ˈprofit ˈon the ˈsale of them.

13 You have made us the ˈscorn of our ˈneighbors, *
    a mockery and de ˈrision to ˈthose a ˈround us.

14 You have made us a byword a ˈmong the ˈnations, *
    a laughing ˈstock a ˈmong the ˈpeoples.

15 My humiliation is ˈdaily be ˈfore me, *
    and ˈshame has ˈcovered my ˈface;

16 Because of the taunts of the ˈmockers and blas ˈphemers, *
    because of the ˈenemy ˈand av ˈenger.

17 All this has 'come upon 'us; *

    yet we have not forgotten you,

    nor have 'we be'trayed your 'covenant.

18 Our heart 'never turned 'back, *

    nor did our 'footsteps 'stray from your 'path;

†19 Though you thrust us down into a 'place of 'misery, *

    and covered us 'over with 'de̋ep 'darkness.

20 If we have forgotten the 'Name of our 'God, *

    or stretched out our 'hands to some 'stränge 'god,

21 Will not God 'find it 'out? *

    for he knows the 'secrets 'of the 'heart.

22 Indeed, for your sake we are killed 'all the day 'long; *

    we are ac'counted as 'sheep for the 'slaughter.

23 Awake, O Lord! 'why are you 'sleeping? *

    Arise! 'do not re'ject us for 'ever.

24 Why have you 'hidden your 'face *

    and forgotten our af'fliction 'and op'pression?

25 We sink 'down into the 'dust; *

    our 'body 'cleaves to the 'ground.

†26 Rise 'up, and 'help us, *

    and save us, for the 'sake of your 'steadfast 'love.

Psalm 45 *Eructavit cor meum*

96
Matthew Camidge

97
Ivor Algernon Atkins

1 My heart is stirring with a noble song;
let me recite what I have ˈfashioned for the ˈking; *
my tongue shall be the ˈpen of a ˈskilled ˈwriter,

2 You are the ˈfairest of ˈmen; *
grace flows from your lips,
because ˈGod has ˈblessed you for ˈever.

3 Strap your sword upon your thigh, O ˈmighty ˈwarrior, *
in your ˈpride and ˈin your ˈmajesty.

4 Ride out and conquer in the ˈcause of ˈtruth *
—ˈand for the ˈsake of ˈjustice.

5 Your right hand will show you ˈmarvelous ˈthings; *
your arrows are very ˈsharp, O ˈmighty ˈwarrior.

6 The peoples are ˈfalling at your ˈfeet, *
and the king's ˈenemies are ˈlosing ˈheart.

7 Your throne, O God, endures for ˈever and ˈever, *
a scepter of righteousness is the scepter of your kingdom;
you love ˈrighteousness and ˈhate in ˈiquity.

8 Therefore God, your ˈGod, has a ˈnointed you *
with the oil of ˈgladness a ˈbove your ˈfellows.

9 All your garments are fragrant with myrrh, 'aloes, and 'cassia, *
 and the music of strings from ivory 'palaces 'makes you 'glad.

10 Kings' daughters stand among the 'ladies of the 'court; *
 on your right hand is the queen,
 a 'dorned with the 'gold of 'Ophir.

11 "Hear, O daughter; consider and 'listen 'closely; *
 forget your 'people and your 'father's house.

12 The king will have 'pleasure in your 'beauty; *
 he is your master; 'therefore 'do him 'honor.

13 The people of Tyre are 'here with a 'gift; *
 the rich among the 'people 'seek your 'favor."

14 All glorious is the princess 'as she 'enters; *
 her 'gown is 'cloth-of-'gold.

15 In embroidered apparel she is 'brought to the 'king; *
 after her the bridesmaids 'follow 'in pro 'cession.

16 With joy and gladness 'they are 'brought, *
 and enter into the 'palace 'of the 'king.

17 "In place of fathers, O king, 'you shall have 'sons; *
 you shall make them 'princes over 'all the 'earth.

18 I will make your name to be remembered
 from one gene 'ration to an 'other; *
 therefore nations will 'praise you for 'ever and 'ever."

Psalm 46 *Deus noster refugium*

98   *Martin Luther*

100   *Benjamin Hutto*

Setting 1: #98–99; setting 2: #100.

1 God is our ⌐refuge and ˈstrength, *
   a very ˈpresent ˈhelp in ˈtrouble.

2 Therefore we will not fear, though the ˈearth be ˈmoved, *
   and though the mountains be toppled ⌐into the ˈdepths of the ˈsea;

3 Though its waters ˈrage and ˈfoam, *
   and though the mountains ˈtremble ˈat its ˈtumult.

4 The LORD of ˈhosts is ˈwith us; *
   the God of ˈJacob ˈis our ˈstronghold.

5 There is a river whose streams make glad the ˈcity of ˈGod, *
   the holy habi ˈtation of the ˈMöst ˈHigh.

6 God is in the midst of her;
   she shall not be ˈover ˈthrown; *
   God shall ˈhelp her at the ˈbreak of ˈday.

99

Martin Luther (Melody in alto)

100

Benjamin Hutto

7 The nations make much ado, and the 'kingdoms are 'shaken; *
   God has spoken, and the 'earth shall 'melt a'way.

8 The LORD of 'hosts is 'with us; *
   the God of 'Jacob 'is our 'stronghold.

In setting 1, return to chant #98

9 Come now and look upon the 'works of the 'LORD, *
   what awesome 'things he has 'done on 'earth.

10 It is he who makes war to cease in 'all the 'world; *
   he breaks the bow, and shatters the spear,
   and 'burns the 'shields with 'fire.

11 "Be still, then, and know that 'I am 'God; *
   I will be exalted among the nations;
   I will be ex'alted 'in the 'earth."

12 The LORD of 'hosts is 'with us; *
   the God of 'Jacob 'is our 'stronghold.

Psalm 47   *Omnes gentes, plaudite*

101   *John Davy*

102   *Thomas Tertius Noble*

1 Clap your hands, 'all you 'peoples; *
    shout to 'God with a 'cry of 'joy.

2 For the LORD Most 'High is to be 'feared; *
    he is the great 'King over 'all the 'earth.

3 He subdues the 'peoples 'under us, *
    and the 'nations 'under our 'feet.

4 He chooses our in 'heritance 'for us, *
    the pride of 'Jacob 'whom he 'loves.

5 God has gone 'up with a 'shout, *
    the 'LORD with the 'sound of the 'ram's-horn.

6 Sing praises to 'God, sing 'praises; *
    sing 'praises to our 'King, sing 'praises.

7 For God is King of 'all the 'earth; *
    sing 'praises with 'all your 'skill.

8 God reigns 'over the 'nations; *
    God 'sits upon his 'holy 'throne.

9 The nobles of the peoples have 'gathered to 'gether *
    with the 'people of the 'God of 'Abraham.

10 The rulers of the earth be 'long to 'God, *
    and 'he is 'highly ex 'alted.

92

Psalm 48 *Magnus Dominus*

103

William Crotch

104

Edwin George Monk

1 Great is the LORD, and 'highly to be 'praised; *
   in the city of our 'God is his 'holy 'hill.

2 Beautiful and lofty, the joy of all the earth, is the 'hill of 'Zion, *
   the very center of the world and the 'city of the 'grëat 'King.

3 God is 'in her 'citadels; *
   he is 'known to be her 'süre 'refuge.

4 Behold, the kings of the 'earth as 'sembled *
   and 'marched 'forward to 'gether.

5 They 'looked and were as 'tounded; *
   they re 'treated and 'fled in 'terror.

6 Trembling 'seized them 'there; *
   they writhed like a woman in childbirth,
   like ships of the 'sea when the 'east wind 'shatters them.

7 As we have heard, so have we seen,
   in the city of the LORD of hosts, in the 'city of our 'God; *
   God has es 'tablished 'her for 'ever.

8 We have waited in silence on your loving 'kindness, O 'God, *
   in the 'midst 'of your 'temple.

103

William Crotch

104

Edwin George Monk

9 Your praise, like your Name, O God, reaches to the ' wörld's ' end; *
   your right ' hand is ' full of ' justice.

10 Let Mount Zion be glad
    and the cities of ' Judah re ' joice, *
    be ' cause of ' yöur ' judgments.

11 Make the circuit of Zion;
    walk ' round a ' bout her; *
    count the ' number ' of her ' towers.

12 Consider well her bulwarks;
    ex ' amine her ' strongholds; *
    that ' you may tell ' those who come ' after.

†13 This God is our God for ' ever and ' ever; *
    he shall be our ' guide for ' ever ' more.

Psalm 49   *Audite haec, omnes*

105
Cambridge Chant

106
Joseph Barnby

1 Hear this, all you peoples;
    hearken, all you who ˈdwell in the ˈworld, *
        you of high degree and low, ˈrich and ˈpoor to ˈgether.

2 My mouth shall ˈspeak of ˈwisdom, *
        and my heart shall ˈmeditate on ˈunder ˈstanding.

3 I will incline my ˈear to a ˈproverb *
        and set forth my ˈriddle up ˈon the ˈharp.

4 Why should I be afraid in ˈevil ˈdays, *
        when the wickedness of ˈthose at my ˈheels sur ˈrounds me,

5 The wickedness of those who put their ˈtrust in their ˈgoods, *
        and ˈboast of their ˈgrëat ˈriches?

6 We can never ˈransom our ˈselves, *
        or deliver to ˈGod the ˈprice of our ˈlife;

7 For the ransom of our ˈlife is so ˈgreat, *
        that we should never ˈhave e ˈnough to ˈpay it,

8 In order to live for ˈever and ˈever, *
        and ˈnever ˈsee the ˈgrave.

95

105

Cambridge Chant

106

Joseph Barnby

9 For we see that the wise die also;
   like the dull and ˈstupid they ˈperish *
      and leave their ˈwealth to ˈthose who come ˈafter them.

10 Their graves shall be their homes for ever,
   their dwelling places from generation to ˈgene ˈration, *
      though they call the ˈlands after ˈtheir own ˈnames.

11 Even though honored, they cannot ˈlive for ˈever; *
   they are ˈlike the ˈbeasts that ˈperish.

12 Such is the way of those who foolishly ˈtrust in them ˈselves, *
   and the end of those who de ˈlight in their ˈown ˈwords.

13 Like a flock of sheep they are destined to die;
   ˈDeath is their ˈshepherd; *
      they go down ˈstraightway ˈto the ˈgrave.

14 Their form shall ˈwaste a ˈway, *
   and the land of the ˈdead shall ˈbe their ˈhome.

15 But God will ˈransom my ˈlife; *
   he will ˈsnatch me from the ˈgrasp of ˈdeath.

16 Do not be envious when ˈsome become ˈrich, *
   or when the ˈgrandeur of their ˈhouse in ˈcreases;

17 For they will carry nothing a'way at their death, *
  nor'will their'grandeur'follow them.

18 Though they thought highly of them'selves while they'lived, *
  and were'praised for'their suc'cess,

19 They shall join the'company of their'forebears, *
  who will'never see the'light a'gain.

20 Those who are honored, but have'no under'standing, *
  are'like the'beasts that'perish.

Psalm 50   *Deus deorum*

107
Jonathan Battishill

108
Henry Smart

Setting 1: #107; setting 2: #108–109

1 The LORD, the God of'gods, has'spoken; *
  he has called the earth from the'rising of the'sun to its'setting.

2 Out of Zion,'perfect in its'beauty, *
  God re'veals him'self in'glory.

3 Our God will come and'will not keep'silence; *
  before him there is a consuming flame,
  and round a'bout him a'raging'storm.

4 He calls the heavens and the'earth from a'bove *
  to witness the'judgment'of his'people.

107

Jonathan Battishill

108

Henry Smart

5 "Gather before me my'loyal'followers, *
   those who have made a covenant with'me and'sealed it with'sacrifice."

6 Let the heavens declare the'rightness of his'cause; *
   for'God him'self is'judge.

7 Hear, O my people, and I will speak:
   "O Israel, I will bear'witness a'gainst you; *
   for'I am'God, your'God.

8 I do not accuse you be'cause of your'sacrifices; *
   your'offerings are'always be'fore me.

9 I will take no bull-calf'from your'stalls, *
   nor'he-goats'out of your'pens;

10 For all the beasts of the'forest are'mine, *
   the herds in their'thousands up'on the'hills.

11 I know every'bird in the'sky, *
   and the creatures of the'fields are'in my'sight.

12 If I were hungry, I'would not'tell you, *
   for the whole world is'mine and'all that is'in it.

†13 Do you think I eat the'flesh of'bulls, *
   or'drink the'blood of'goats?

98

14 Offer to God a 'sacrifice of 'thanksgiving *
 and make good your 'vows to the 'Möst 'High.

15 Call upon me in the 'day of 'trouble; *
 I will de 'liver you, and 'you shall 'honor me."

107 *Jonathan Battishill*

109 *Samuel Wesley*

16 But to the 'wicked God 'says: *
 "Why do you recite my statutes,
 and take my 'covenant up 'on your 'lips;

17 Since you re 'füse 'discipline, *
 and toss my 'words be 'hind your 'back?

18 When you see a thief, you 'make him your 'friend, *
 and you 'cast in your 'lot with ad 'ulterers.

19 You have loosed your 'lips for 'evil, *
 and 'harnessed your 'tongue to a 'lie.

20 You are always speaking 'evil of your 'brother *
 and 'slandering your 'own mother's 'son.

21 These things you have done, and I 'këpt 'still, *
 and you 'thought that 'I am like 'you."

107   *Jonathan Battishill*

109   *Samuel Wesley*

22 "I have made my ' accu ' sation; *
   I have put my case in ' order be ' fore your ' eyes.

23 Consider this well, you who for ' gët ' God, *
   lest I rend you and ' there be ' none to de ' liver you.

†24 Whoever offers me the sacrifice of thanksgiving ' honors ' me; *
   but to those who keep in my way will I ' show the sal ' vation of ' God."

110

Matthew Camidge

John Stainer

111

1 Have mercy on me, O God, according to your'loving⌐kindness; *
   in your great compassion'blot out'my of'fenses.

2 Wash me through and'through from my'wickedness *
   and'cleanse me'from my'sin.

3 For I'know my trans'gressions, *
   and my'sin is'ever be'fore me.

4 Against you'only have I'sinned *
   and done what is'evil'in your'sight.

5 And so you are justified'when you'speak *
   and'upright'in your'judgment.

6 Indeed, I have been'wicked from my'birth, *
   a'sinner from my'mother's'womb.

7 For behold, you look for truth'deep with'in me, *
   and will make me under'ständ'wisdom'secretly.

8 Purge me from my sin, and'I shall be'pure; *
   wash me, and'I shall be'clean in'deed.

110

111

9 Make me hear of ' joy and ' gladness, *
   that the body you have ' broken ' may re ' joice.

10 Hide your ' face from my ' sins *
   and blot ' out all ' my in ' iquities.

11 Create in me a clean ' heart, O ' God, *
   and re ' new a right ' spirit with ' in me.

12 Cast me not a ' way from your ' presence *
   and take not your ' holy ' Spirit ' from me.

13 Give me the joy of your saving ' help a ' gain *
   and sus ' tain me with your ' bountiful ' Spirit.

14 I shall teach your ' ways to the ' wicked, *
   and sinners ' shall re ' turn to ' you.

15 Deliver me from ' death, O ' God, *
   and my tongue shall sing of your righteousness,
   O ' God of ' my sal ' vation.

16 Open my ' lips, O ' Lord, *
   and my ' mouth shall pro ' claim your ' praise.

17 Had you desired it, I would have ' offered ' sacrifice, *
   but you take no de ' light in ' burnt ' offerings.

18 The sacrifice of God is a ' troubled ' spirit; *
   a broken and contrite heart, O ' God, you will ' not des ' pise.

19 Be favorable and 'gracious to 'Zion, *
    and re'build the 'walls of Jer'usalem.

20 Then you will be pleased with the appointed sacrifices,
    with burnt 'offerings and ob'lations; *
    then shall they offer young 'bullocks up'on your 'altar.

Psalm 52 *Quid gloriaris?*

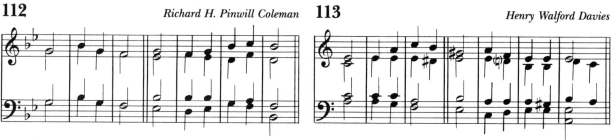

112 *Richard H. Pinwill Coleman*   **113** *Henry Walford Davies*

Setting 1: #112; setting 2: #113–114

1 You tyrant, why do you 'boast of 'wickedness *
    against the 'godly 'all day 'long?

2 You plot ruin;
    your tongue is like a 'sharpened 'razor, *
    O 'worker 'of de'ception.

3 You love evil 'more than 'good *
    and lying 'more than 'speaking the 'truth.

4 You love all 'words that 'hurt, *
    O 'you de'ceitful 'tongue.

5 Oh, that God would de'molish you 'utterly, *
    topple you, and snatch you from your dwelling,
    and root you 'out of the 'land of the 'living!

6 The righteous shall 'see and 'tremble, *
    and 'they shall 'laugh at him, 'saying,

7 "This is the one who did not take 'God for a 'refuge, *
    but trusted in great wealth
    'and re'lied upon 'wickedness."

103

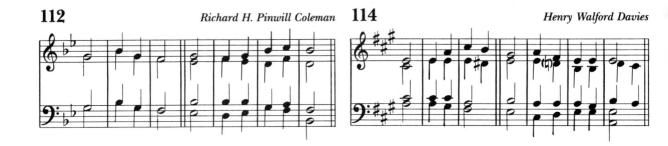

112 *Richard H. Pinwill Coleman* **114** *Henry Walford Davies*

8 But I am like a green olive tree in the ˈhouse of ˈGod; *
  I trust in the mercy of ˈGod for ˈever and ˈever.

9 I will give you thanks for ˈwhat you have ˈdone *
  and declare the goodness of your Name in the ˈpresence ˈof the ˈgodly.

Psalm 53
Dixit insipiens

115 — John Blow

116 — John Goss

1 The fool has said in his heart, "There⁣|is no|God." *
  All are corrupt and commit abominable acts;
  there is|none who does|any|good.

2 God looks down from heaven up|on us|all, *
  to see if there is any who is wise,
  if there is|one who|seeks after|God.

3 Every one has proved faithless;
  all a|like have turned|bad; *
  there is none who does|good;|no, not|one.

4 Have they no knowledge, those|evil|doers *
  who eat up my people like bread
  and|do not|call upon|God?

5 See how greatly they tremble,
  such trembling as|never|was; *
  for God has scattered the bones of the enemy;
  they are put to|shame, because|God has re|jected them.

6 Oh, that Israel's deliverance would come|out of|Zion! *
  when God restores the fortunes of his people
  Jacob will re|joice and|Israel be|glad.

105

Psalm 54   *Deus, in nomine*

117   *John Goss*   **118**   *C. Hylton Stewart*

1 Save me, O'God, by your'Name; *
   in your'might, de'fend my'cause.

2 Hear my'prayer, O'God; *
   give ear to the'words'of my'mouth.

3 For the arrogant have risen up against me,
   and the ruthless have'sought my'life, *
   those who have'no re'gard for'God.

4 Behold,'God is my'helper; *
   it is the'Lord who sus'tains my'life.

5 Render evil to'those who'spy on me; *
   in your'faithful'ness, de'stroy them.

6 I will offer you a'freewill'sacrifice *
   and praise your Name, O'LORD, for'it is'good.

7 For you have rescued me from'every'trouble, *
   and my eye has seen the'ruin'of my'foes.

Psalm 55 *Exaudi, Deus*

119

Edward John Hopkins

120

Ray Francis Brown

1 Hear my ꞌprayer, O ꞌGod; *
  do not hide yourꞌself from ꞌmy peꞌtition.

2 Listen to ꞌme and ꞌanswer me; *
  I have no ꞌpeace, beꞌcause of my ꞌcares.

3 I am shaken by the ꞌnoise of the ꞌenemy *
  and by the ꞌpressure ꞌof the ꞌwicked;

4 For they have cast an evil ꞌspell upꞌon me *
  and are ꞌset aꞌgainst me in ꞌfury.

5 My heart ꞌquakes withꞌin me, *
  and the terrors of ꞌdeath have ꞌfallen upꞌon me.

6 Fear and trembling have ꞌcöme ꞌover me, *
  and ꞌhorror ꞌoverꞌwhelms me.

7 And I said, "Oh, that I had ꞌwings like a ꞌdove! *
  I would fly aꞌway and ꞌbe at ꞌrest.

8 I would flee to a ꞌfar-off ꞌplace *
  and make my ꞌlodging ꞌin the ꞌwilderness.

Edward John Hopkins

Ray Francis Brown

9 I would |hasten to es|cape *
   from the |stormy |wind and |tempest."

10 Swallow them up, O LORD;
   con|found their |speech; *
      for I have seen |violence and |strife in the |city.

11 Day and night the watchmen make their rounds up|on her |walls, *
   but trouble and |misery are |in the |midst of her.

12 There is cor|ruption at her |heart; *
   her streets are never free of op|pression |and de|ceit.

13 For had it been an adversary who taunted me,
   then I|could have |borne it; *
      or had it been an enemy who vaunted himself against me,
      then |I could have |hidden from |him.

14 But it was you, a man after my |own |heart, *
   my companion, my |own fa|miliar |friend.

15 We took sweet |counsel to|gether, *
   and walked with the |throng in the |house of |God.

16 Let death come upon them suddenly;
  let them go down a'live into the 'grave; *
    for wickedness is in their dwellings, 'in their 'very 'midst.

17 But I will 'call upon 'God, *
    and the 'LORD 'will de'liver me.

18 In the evening, in the morning, and at noonday,
  I will com'plain and la'ment, *
    and 'he will 'hear my 'voice.

19 He will bring me safely back from the battle 'waged a'gainst me; *
    for 'there are 'many who 'fight me.

20 God, who is enthroned of old, will hear me and 'bring them 'down; *
    they never change; 'they do 'not fear 'God.

21 My companion stretched forth his hand a'gainst his 'comrade; *
    — 'he has 'broken his 'covenant.

22 His speech is 'softer than 'butter, *
    but 'war is 'in his 'heart.

23 His words are 'smoother than 'oil, *
    but 'they are 'dräwn 'swords.

24 Cast your burden upon the LORD,
  and 'he will sus'tain you; *
    he will never 'let the 'righteous 'stumble.

25 For you will bring the 'bloodthirsty and de'ceitful *
    down to the 'pit of de'struction, O 'God.

26 They shall not live out 'half their 'days, *
    but I will 'put my 'trust in 'you.

Psalm 56 *Miserere mei, Deus*

121

William Crotch

122

Henry G. Ley

1 Have mercy on me, O God,
    for my ' enemies are ' hounding me; *
        all day long ' they as ' sault and op ' press me.

2 They hound me ' all the day ' long; *
    truly there are many who fight a ' gainst me, ' O Most ' High.

3 Whenever ' I am a ' fraid, *
    I will ' put my ' trust in ' you.

4 In God, whose word I praise,
    in God I trust and will ' not be a ' fraid, *
        for ' what can ' flesh ' do to me?

5 All day long they ' damage my ' cause; *
    their only ' thought is to ' do me ' evil.

6 They band together; they ' lie in ' wait; *
    they spy upon my footsteps;
        be ' cause they ' seek my ' life.

7 Shall they escape de ' spite their ' wickedness? *
    O God, in your ' anger, cast ' down the ' peoples.

8 You have noted my lamentation;
    put my ' tears into your ' bottle; *
        are they not re ' corded ' in your ' book?

110

9 Whenever I call upon you, my enemies will be ǀ put to ǀ flight; *
 this I know, for ǀ God is ǀ on my ǀ side.

10 In God the LORD, whose word I praise,
 in God I trust and will ǀ not be a ǀ fraid, *
 for ǀ what can ǀ mortals ǀ do to me?

11 I am bound by the vow I made to ǀ you, O ǀ God; *
 I will pre ǀ sent to ǀ you thank ǀ offerings;

12 For you have rescued my soul from death and my ǀ feet from ǀ stumbling, *
 that I may walk before ǀ God in the ǀ light of the ǀ living.

Psalm 57   *Miserere mei, Deus*

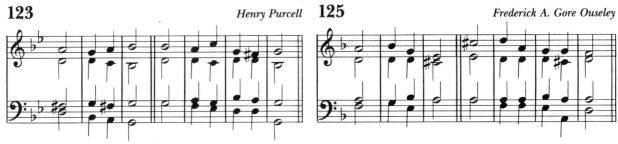

123   Henry Purcell **125**   Frederick A. Gore Ouseley

Setting 1: #123–124; setting 2: #125–126.

1 Be merciful to me, O God, be merciful,
   for I have taken⎤refuge in⎤you; *
       in the shadow of your wings will I take refuge
       until this time of⎤trouble⎤has gone⎤by.

2 I will call upon the⎤Most High⎤God, *
       the⎤God who main⎤tains my⎤cause.

3 He will send from heaven and save me;
   he will confound those who⎤trample up⎤on me; *
       God will send⎤forth his⎤love and his⎤faithfulness.

4 I lie in the midst of lions that de⎤vour the⎤people; *
       their teeth are spears and arrows,
       their⎤tongue a⎤shärp⎤sword.

5 They have laid a net for my feet,
   and I am⎤bowed⎤low; *
       they have dug a pit before me,
       but have⎤fallen into⎤it them⎤selves.

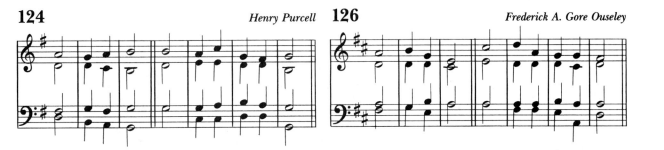

6 Exalt yourself above the ˈheavens, O ˈGod, *
   and your ˈglory over ˈall the ˈearth.

7 My heart is firmly fixed, O God, my ˈheart is ˈfixed; *
   I will ˈsing and ˈmäke ˈmelody.

8 Wake up, my spirit,
   awake, ˈlute and ˈharp; *
   I my ˈself will ˈwaken the ˈdawn.

9 I will confess you among the ˈpeoples, O ˈLORD; *
   I will sing praise to ˈyou a ˈmong the ˈnations.

10 For your loving-kindness is ˈgreater than the ˈheavens, *
   and your faithfulness ˈreaches ˈto the ˈclouds.

11 Exalt yourself above the ˈheavens, O ˈGod, *
   and your ˈglory over ˈall the ˈearth.

Psalm 58   *Si vere utique*

127   *Luke Flintoff*

128   *William Crotch*

1 Do you indeed decree ˈrighteousness, you ˈrulers? *
   do you ˈjudge the ˈpeoples with ˈequity?

2 No; you devise ˈevil in your ˈhearts, *
   and your hands deal out ˈviolence ˈin the ˈland.

3 The wicked are perˈverse from the ˈwomb; *
   liars go aˈsträy ˈfrom their ˈbirth.

4 They are as ˈvenomous as a ˈserpent, *
   they are like the deaf ˈadder which ˈstops its ˈears,

5 Which does not heed the ˈvoice of the ˈcharmer, *
   no ˈmatter how ˈskillful his ˈcharming.

6 O God, break their ˈteeth in their ˈmouths; *
   pull the fangs of the ˈyoüng ˈlions, O ˈLORD.

7 Let them vanish like water that ˈrüns ˈoff; *
   let them ˈwither like ˈtrodden ˈgrass.

8 Let them be like the snail that ˈmelts ˈaway, *
   like a stillborn child that ˈnever ˈsees the ˈsun.

9 Before they bear fruit, let them be cut'down like a'brier; *
   like thorns and thistles'let them be'swept a'way.

10 The righteous will be glad when they'see the'vengeance; *
   they will bathe their'feet in the'blood of the'wicked.

†11 And they will say,
   "Surely, there is a re'ward for the righteous; *
   surely, there is a'God who'rules in the'earth."

Psalm 59   *Eripe me de inimicis*

129

William Beale

131

Charles Villiers Stanford

Setting 1: #129–130; setting 2: #131–132

1 Rescue me from my'enemies, O'God; *
   protect me from'those who rise'up a'gainst me.

2 Rescue me from'evil'doers *
   and save me from'those who'thirst for my'blood.

3 See how they lie in wait for my life,
   how the mighty gather to'gether a'gainst me; *
   not for any offense or'fault of'mine, O'LORD.

4 Not because of any'guilt of'mine *
   they run and pre'pare them'selves for'battle.

129

William Beale

131

Charles Villiers Stanford

5 Rouse yourself, come to my | side, and | see; *
    for you, LORD God of | hosts, are | Israel's | God.

6 Awake, and punish | all the un | godly; *
    show no mercy to | those who are | faithless and | evil.

7 They go to and | fro in the | evening; *
    they snarl like dogs and | run a | bout the | city.

8 Behold, they boast with their mouths,
    and taunts are | on their | lips; *
    "For | who," they | say, "will | hear us?"

†9 But you, O | LORD, you | laugh at them; *
    you laugh | all the un | godly to | scorn.

10 My eyes are fixed on you, | O my | Strength; *
    for you, O | Göd, | are my | stronghold.

11 My merciful God | comes to | meet me; *
    God will let me look in | triumph | on my | enemies.

12 Slay them, O God, lest my | people for | get; *
    send them reeling by your might
    and put them | down, O | Lord our | shield.

13 For the sins of their mouths, for the words of their lips,
    for the cursing and | lies that they | utter, *
    let them be | caüght | in their | pride.

14 Make an end of them ' in your ' wrath; *
　　make an end of them, and ' they shall ' be no ' more.

15 Let everyone know that ' God rules in ' Jacob, *
　　and to the ' ends ' of the ' earth.

16 They go to and ' fro in the ' evening; *
　　they snarl like dogs and ' run a'bout the ' city.

17 They ' forage for ' food, *
　　and ' if they are not ' filled, they ' howl.

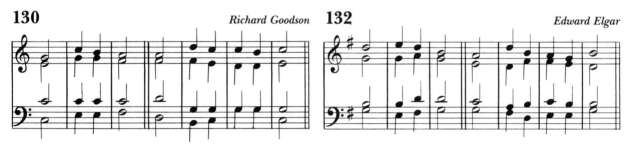

130　　　　　　　　　*Richard Goodson*　　**132**　　　　　　　　*Edward Elgar*

18 For my part, I will ' sing of your ' strength; *
　　I will celebrate your ' love ' in the ' morning;

19 For you have ' become my ' stronghold, *
　　a ' refuge in the ' day of my ' trouble.

20 To you, O my ' Strength, will I ' sing; *
　　for you, O God, are my stronghold ' and my ' merciful ' God.

Psalm 60 *Deus, repulisti nos*

133

John Goss

134

Julius Harrison

Setting 1: #133; setting 2: #134–135

1 O God, you have cast us'off and'broken us; *
 you have been angry;
 oh, take us'back to'you a'gain.

2 You have shaken the earth and'split it'open; *
 repair the'cracks in it,'for it'totters.

3 You have made your'people know'hardship; *
 you have given us'wine that'makes us'stagger.

4 You have set up a banner for'those who'fear you, *
 to be a refuge from the'power'of the'bow.

†5 Save us by your right'hand and'answer us, *
 that those who are dear to'you may'be de'livered.

133

135

Julius Harrison

6 God spoke from his holy⎸place and⎸said: *
   "I will exult and parcel out Shechem;
   I will di⎸vide the⎸valley of⎸Succoth.

7 Gilead is mine and Ma⎸nasseh is⎸mine; *
   Ephraim is my⎸helmet and⎸Judah my⎸scepter.

†8 Moab is my wash-basin,
   on Edom I throw down my⎸sandal to⎸claim it, *
   and over Philistia⎸will I⎸shout in⎸triumph."

9 Who will lead me into the⎸strŏng⎸city? *
   who will⎸bring me⎸into⎸Edom?

10 Have you not cast us⎸off, O⎸God? *
   you no longer go⎸out, O⎸God, with our⎸armies.

11 Grant us your help a⎸gainst the⎸enemy, *
   for⎸vain is the⎸help of⎸man.

12 With God we will do⎸valiant⎸deeds, *
   and he shall tread our⎸enemies⎸under⎸foot.

Psalm 61 *Exaudi, Deus*

136

Joseph Leopold Roeckel

137

Jonathan Battishill

1 Hear my ' cry, O ' God, *
   and ' listen ' to my ' prayer.

2 I call upon you from the ends of the earth
   with ' heaviness in my ' heart; *
   set me upon the ' rock that is ' higher than ' I.

3 For you have ' been my ' refuge, *
   a strong ' tower a ' gainst the ' enemy.

4 I will dwell in your ' house for ' ever; *
   I will take refuge under the ' cover ' of your ' wings.

5 For you, O God, have ' heard my ' vows; *
   you have granted me the heritage of ' those who ' fear your ' Name.

6 Add length of days to the ' king's ' life; *
   let his years extend over ' many ' gene ' rations.

7 Let him sit enthroned before ' God for ' ever; *
   bid love and ' faithfulness ' watch ' over him.

8 So will I always sing the ' praise of your ' Name, *
   and day by day I ' will ful ' fill my ' vows.

Psalm 62 *Nonne Deo?*

138

George Thalben-Ball

139

George Clement Martin

1 For God alone my soul in 'silence'waits; *
   from'him comes'my sal'vation.

2 He alone is my rock and'my sal'vation, *
   my stronghold, so that I'shall not be'greatly'shaken.

3 How long will you assail me to crush me,
   'all of you to'gether, *
   as if you were a leaning'fence, a'toppling'wall?

4 They seek only to bring me down from my'place of'honor; *
   —'lies are their'chief de'light.

5 They'bless with their'lips, *
   but'in their'hearts they'curse.

6 For God alone my soul in'silence'waits; *
   —'truly, my'hope is in'him.

7 He alone is my rock and'my sal'vation, *
   my stronghold,'so that I'shall not be'shaken.

8 In God is my'safety and my'honor; *
   God is my strong'röck'and my'refuge.

138

George Thalben-Ball

139

George Clement Martin

9 Put your trust in him ˈalwaysˌ O ˈpeople, *
    pour out your hearts beˈfore him, for ˈGod is our ˈrefuge.

10 Those of high degree are but a ˈfleeting ˈbreath, *
    even those of low esˈtate canˈnot be ˈtrusted.

11 On the scales they are ˈlighter than a ˈbreath, *
    —ˈall of ˈthem to ˈgether.

12 Put no trust in extortion;
    in robbery take no ˈempty ˈpride; *
    though wealth increase, ˈset not your ˈheart up ˈon it.

13 God has spoken once, ˈtwice have I ˈheard it, *
    that ˈpower be ˈlongs to ˈGod.

14 Steadfast love is ˈyours, O ˈLord, *
    for you repay everyone acˈcording ˈto his ˈdeeds.

Psalm 63 *Deus, Deus meus*

140 *Thomas Jackson*

141 *Jackman*

1 O God, you are my God; ͏eagerly I ͏seek you; *
   my soul thirsts for you, my flesh faints for you,
   as in a barren and dry ͏land where there ͏is no ͏water.

2 Therefore I have gazed upon you in your ͏holy ͏place, *
   that I might be ͏hold your ͏power and your ͏glory.

3 For your loving-kindness is better than ͏life it ͏self; *
   my ͏lips shall ͏give you ͏praise.

4 So will I bless you as ͏long as I ͏live *
   and lift ͏up my ͏hands in your ͏Name.

5 My soul is content, as with ͏marrow and ͏fatness, *
   and my mouth ͏praises you with ͏joyful ͏lips,

6 When I remember you up ͏on my ͏bed, *
   and ͏meditate on ͏you in the ͏night watches.

7 For you have ͏been my ͏helper, *
   and under the shadow of your ͏wings I ͏will re ͏joice.

8 My ͏sŏul ͏clings to you; *
   your ͏right hand ͏holds me ͏fast.

140

Thomas Jackson

141

Jackman

9 May those who seek my 'life to de 'stroy it *
   go 'down into the 'depths of the 'earth;

10 Let them fall upon the 'edge of the 'sword, *
   and 'let them be 'food for 'jackals.

†11 But the king will rejoice in God;
   all those who swear by 'him will be 'glad; *
      for the mouth of 'those who speak 'lies shall be 'stopped.

Psalm 64 *Exaudi, Deus*

142

Joseph Barnby

143*

A   B

Richard Wayne Dirksen

C

A**   1 Hear my voice, O God, when'I com'plain; *
        protect my'life from'fear of the'enemy.

B   2 Hide me from the con'spiracy of the'wicked, *
        from the'mob of'evil'doers.

C   3 They sharpen their'tongue like a'sword, *
        and aim their'bitter'words like'arrows,

A   4 That they may shoot down the'blameless from'ambush; *
        they shoot without'warning and'are not a'fraid.

B   5 They hold fast to their'evil'course; *
        they plan how'they may'hide their'snares.

If the Gloria Patri is sung, the small notes at the end of A should be used as a splice to C. If the Gloria Patri is not sung, sing verse 10 to C, using the splice for verse 9.

**In setting two, these letters indicate the section of the chant to be sung to each verse.*

142

143

A   B

Richard Wayne Dirksen

C

C   6 They say, "Who will see us?
          who will find'out our'crimes? *
          we have thought'out a'perfect'plot."

A   7 The human mind and'heart are a'mystery; *
          but God will loose an arrow at them,
          and'suddenly they'will be'wounded.

B   8 He will make them trip'over their'tongues, *
          and all who'see them will'shake their'heads.

A   9 Everyone will stand in awe and de'clare God's'deeds; *
          they will'recog'nize his'works.

B   †10 The righteous will rejoice in the LORD and'put their'trust in him, *
          and all who are'true of'heart will'glory.

      †*For triple chant*

Psalm 65   *Te decet hymnus*

144

Henry Smart

145

Gerre Hancock

1 You are to be praised, O'God, in'Zion; *
   to you shall'vows be per'formed in Je'rusalem.

2 To you that hear prayer shall'all flesh'come, *
   be'cause of'their trans'gressions.

3 Our sins are'stronger than'we are, *
   but'you will'blot them'out.

4 Happy are they whom you choose
   and draw to your'courts to'dwell there! *
       they will be satisfied by the beauty of your house,
       by the'holiness'of your'temple.

5 Awesome things will you show us in your righteousness,
   O God of'our sal'vation, *
       O Hope of all the ends of the earth
       and of the'seas that are'far a'way.

6 You make fast the'mountains by your'power; *
   they are'girded a'bout with'might.

144

145

Gerre Hancock

7 You still the ‖roaring of the ‖seas, *
   the roaring of their waves,
   and the ‖clamor ‖of the ‖peoples.

8 Those who dwell at the ends of the earth will tremble at
          your ‖marvelous ‖signs; *
   you make the dawn and the ‖dusk to ‖sing for ‖joy.

9 You visit the earth and water it abundantly;
   you make it ‖very ‖plenteous; *
   the river of ‖God is ‖full of ‖water.

10 You pre‖pare the ‖grain, *
   for ‖so you pro‖vide for the ‖earth.

11 You drench the furrows and smooth ‖out the ‖ridges; *
   with heavy rain you soften the ‖ground and ‖bless its ‖increase.

12 You crown the ‖year with your ‖goodness, *
   and your paths ‖over‖flow with ‖plenty.

13 May the fields of the wilderness be ‖rich for ‖grazing, *
   and the ‖hills be ‖clothed with ‖joy.

14 May the meadows cover themselves with flocks,
   and the valleys cloak them‖selves with ‖grain; *
   let them ‖shout for ‖joy and ‖sing.

Psalm 66   *Jubilate Deo*

146   *Charles Villiers Stanford*

147   *John Davy*

1 Be joyful in God, ' all you ' lands; *
    sing the glory of his Name;
    sing the ' glory ' of his ' praise.

2 Say to God, "How ' awesome are your ' deeds! *
    because of your great strength your ' enemies ' cringe be ' fore you.

†3 All the earth bows ' down be ' fore you, *
    sings to ' you, sings ' out your ' Name."

4 Come now and see the ' works of ' God, *
    how wonderful he is in his ' doing ' toward all ' people.

5 He turned the sea into dry land,
    so that they went through the ' water on ' foot, *
    and ' thëre ' we re ' joiced in him.

†6 In his might he rules for ever;
    his eyes keep watch ' over the ' nations; *
    let no ' rebel rise ' up a ' gainst him.

7 Bless our ' God, you ' peoples; *
    make the ' voice of his ' praise to be ' heard;

8 Who holds our ' souls in ' life, *
    and will not al ' low our ' feet to ' slip.

129

146

Charles Villiers Stanford

147

John Davy

9 For you, O⎜God, have⎜proved us; *
   you have tried us⎜just as⎜silver is⎜tried.

10 You brought us⎜into the⎜snare; *
   you laid heavy⎜burdens up⎜on our⎜backs.

†11 You let enemies ride over our heads;
   we went through⎜fire and⎜water; *
     but you brought us out⎜into a⎜place of re⎜freshment.

12 I will enter your house with burnt-offerings
   and will⎜pay you my⎜vows, *
     which I promised with my lips
     and spoke with my⎜mouth when I⎜was in⎜trouble.

13 I will offer you sacrifices of fat beasts
   with the⎜smoke of⎜rams; *
     I will⎜give you⎜oxen and⎜goats.

14 Come and listen, all⎜you who fear⎜God, *
   and I will⎜tell you⎜what he has⎜done for me.

15 I called out to⎜him with my⎜mouth, *
   and his⎜praise was⎜on my⎜tongue.

16 If I had found 'evil in my 'heart, *
    the 'Lord would 'not have 'heard me;

17 But in truth 'God has 'heard me; *
    he has attended to the 'voice 'of my 'prayer.

†18 Blessèd be God, who has not re 'jected my 'prayer, *
    nor with 'held his 'love from 'me.

Psalm 67   *Deus misereatur*

148

George Thalben-Ball

149

Edward Cuthbert Bairstow

Reproduced by permission of Novello and Company, Limited.

1 May God be merciful to 'us and 'bless us, *
    show us the light of his 'counte 'nance and 'come to us.

2 Let your ways be 'known upon 'earth, *
    your saving 'health a 'mong all 'nations.

3 Let the peoples 'praise you, O 'God; *
    let 'all the 'peoples 'praise you.

4 Let the nations be glad and 'sing for 'joy, *
    for you judge the peoples with equity
    and guide all the 'nations 'upon 'earth.

148

George Thalben-Ball

149

Edward Cuthbert Bairstow

5 Let the peoples'praise you, O'God; *
   let'all the'peoples'praise you.

6 The earth has brought'forth her'increase; *
   may God, our'own God,'give us his'blessing.

†7 May God'give us his'blessing, *
   and may all the ends of the'eärth'stand in'awe of him.

Psalm 68   *Exsurgat Deus*

150   *Kellow J. Pye*

151   *David Hurd*

Pedal held throughout
Setting 1: #150; setting 2: #151–152.

1 Let God arise, and let his ⌐enemies be ˈscattered; *
  let those who ˈhate him ˈflee be ˈfore him.

2 Let them vanish like smoke when the wind ˈdrives it a ˈway; *
  as the wax melts at the fire, so let the wicked ˈperish at the
  ˈpresence of ˈGod.

3 But let the righteous be glad and re ˈjoice before ˈGod; *
  let them ˈalso be ˈmerry and ˈjoyful.

4 Sing to God, sing praises to his Name;
  exalt him who ˈrides upon the ˈheavens; *
  YAHWEH is his ˈName, re ˈjoice be ˈfore him!

5 Father of orphans, de ˈfender of ˈwidows, *
  God in his ˈholy ˈhabi ˈtation!

6 God gives the solitary a home and brings forth prisoners ˈinto ˈfreedom; *
  but the ˈrebels shall ˈlive in dry ˈplaces.

7 O God, when you went forth be ˈfore your ˈpeople, *
  when you ˈmarched ˈthrough the ˈwilderness,

8 The earth shook, and the skies poured down rain,
  at the presence of God, the ˈGod of ˈSinai, *
  at the presence of ˈGod, the ˈGod of ˈIsrael.

150

Kellow J. Pye

151

David Hurd

Pedal held throughout

9 You sent a gracious rain, O God, upon ' your in ' heritance; *
  you refreshed the ' land when ' it was ' weary.

10 Your people ' found their ' home in it; *
   in your goodness, O God, you have ' made pro ' vision for the ' poor.

11 The Lord ' gave the ' word; *
   great was the company of ' women who ' bore the ' tidings:

12 "Kings with their armies are ' fleeing a ' way; *
   the women at ' home are di ' viding the ' spoils."

13 Though you lingered a ' mong the ' sheepfolds, *
   you shall be like a dove whose wings are covered with silver,
   whose ' feathers are like ' green ' gold.

14 When the Almighty ' scattered ' kings, *
   it was like ' snöw ' falling in ' Zalmon.

15 O mighty mountain, O ' hill of ' Bashan! *
   O rugged ' mountain, O ' hill of ' Bashan!

16 Why do you look with envy, O rugged mountain,
   at the hill which God ' chose for his ' resting place? *
   truly, the ' LORD will ' dwell there for ' ever.

17 The chariots of God are twenty thousand,
even ˈthousands of ˈthousands; *
   the Lord comes in ˈholiˈness from ˈSinai.

18 You have gone up on high and led captivity captive;
you have received gifts even ˈfrom your ˈenemies, *
   that the LORD ˈGod might ˈdwell aˈmong them.

19 Blessed be the Lord ˈday by ˈday, *
   the God of our salˈvation, who ˈbears our ˈburdens.

20 He is our God, the ˈGod of our salˈvation; *
   God is the LORD, by ˈwhom we esˈcäpe ˈdeath.

150   *Kellow J. Pye*

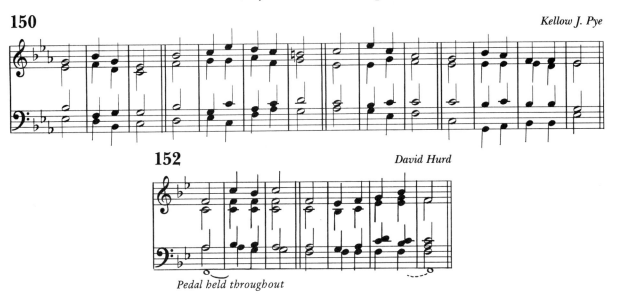

152   *David Hurd*

Pedal held throughout

21 God shall crush the ˈheads of his ˈenemies, *
   and the hairy scalp of those who ˈgo on ˈstill in their ˈwickedness.

22 The LORD has said, "I will bring them ˈback from ˈBashan; *
   I will bring them ˈback from the ˈdepths of the ˈsea;

†23 That your foot may be ˈdipped in ˈblood, *
   the tongues of your ˈdogs in the ˈblood of your ˈenemies."

Tune change

150

Kellow J. Pye

151

David Hurd

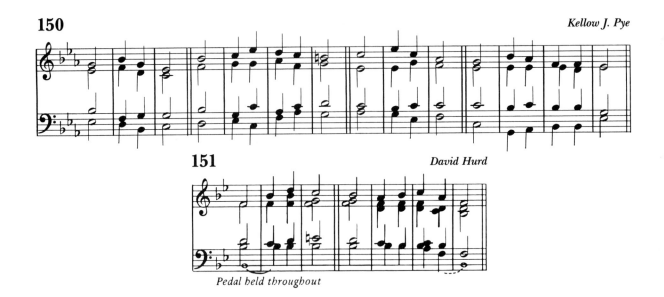

Pedal held throughout

24 They see your pro'cession, O'God, *
   your procession into the'sanctuary, my'God and my'King.

25 The singers go before, mu'sicians follow'after, *
   in the midst of maidens'playing up'on the'hand-drums.

26 Bless God in the'congre'gation; *
   bless the LORD, you that'are of the'fountain of'Israel.

27 There is Benjamin, least of the tribes, at the head;
   the princes of'Judah in a'company; *
   and the'princes of'Zebulon and'Naphtali.

28 Send forth your'strength, O'God; *
   establish, O'Göd,'what you have'wrought for us.

29 Kings shall bring'gifts to'you, *
   for your'temple's sake'at Jer'usalem.

30 Rebuke the wild'beast of the'reeds, *
   and the peoples, a'herd of wild'bulls with its'calves.

31 Trample down those who'lust after'silver; *
   scatter the'peoples that de'light in'war.

†32 Let tribute be'brought out of'Egypt; *
   let Ethiopia stretch'out her'hands to'God.

33 Sing to God, O ˈkingdoms of theˈearth; *
    singˈpraisesˈto theˈLord.

34 He rides in the heavens, theˈancientˈheavens; *
    he sends forth hisˈvoice, hisˈmightyˈvoice.

35 Ascribeˈpower toˈGod; *
    his majesty is over Israel;
    hisˈstrength isˈin theˈskies.

36 How wonderful is God in hisˈholyˈplaces! *
    the God of Israel giving strength and power to his people!
    ˈBlessèdˈbëˈGod!

Psalm 69   *Salvum me fac*

153

Ray Francis Brown

154

Jonathan Battishill

Setting 1: #153; setting 2: #154–155

1 Save ' me, O ' God, *
   for the waters have ' risen ' up to my ' neck.

2 I am sinking in ' dëep ' mire, *
   and there is no firm ' groünd ' for my ' feet.

†3 I have come into ' dëep ' waters, *
   and the ' torrent ' washes ' over me.

4 I have grown weary with my crying;
   my ' throat is in ' flamed; *
   my eyes have failed from ' looking ' for my ' God.

5 Those who hate me without a cause are more than the hairs of my head;
   my lying foes who would de ' stroy me are ' mighty. *
   Must I then give ' back what I ' never ' stole?

6 O God, you ' know my ' foolishness, *
   and my ' faults are not ' hidden from ' you.

7 Let not those who hope in you be put to shame through
      me, Lord ' GOD of ' hosts; *

let not those who seek you be disgraced because
      of ' me, O ' God of ' Israel.

8 Surely, for your sake have I ' suffered re ' proach, *

and ' shame has ' covered my ' face.

9 I have become a stranger to my ' own ' kindred, *

an ' alien to my ' mother's ' children.

10 Zeal for your house has ' eaten me ' up; *

the scorn of those who scorn ' you has ' fallen up ' on me.

11 I humbled my ' self with ' fasting, *

but that was ' turned to ' my re ' proach.

12 I put on ' sack-cloth ' also, *

and be ' came a ' byword a ' mong them.

13 Those who sit at the gate ' murmur a ' gainst me, *

and the ' drunkards make ' songs a ' bout me.

153

Ray Francis Brown

155

Edmund T. Chipp

153

Ray Francis Brown

155

Edmund T. Chipp

14 But as for me, this is my'prayer to'you, *
    at the'time you have'set, O'LORD:

15 "In your great'mercy, O'God, *
    answer me with'your un'failing'help.

16 Save me from the mire; do not'let me'sink; *
    let me be rescued from those who hate me
    and'out of the'dëep'waters.

17 Let not the torrent of waters wash over me,
    neither let the deep'swallow me'up; *
    do not let the Pit'shut its'mouth up'on me.

†18 Answer me, O LORD, for your'love is'kind; *
    in your'great com'passion,'turn to me."

19 "Hide not your'face from your'servant; *
    be swift and answer me, for'I am'in dis'tress.

20 Draw near to'me and re'deem me; *
    be'cause of my'enemies de'liver me.

21 You know my reproach, my ˈshame, and my disˈhonor; *
    my adversaries are ˈall ˈin your ˈsight."

22 Reproach has broken my heart, and it ˈcannot be ˈhealed; *
    I looked for sympathy, but there was none,
    for comforters, but ˈI could ˈfind ˈno one.

†23 They gave me ˈgall to ˈeat, *
    and when I was thirsty, they ˈgave me ˈvinegar to ˈdrink.

153

Ray Francis Brown

154

Jonathan Battishill

24 Let the table before them ˈbe a ˈtrap *
    and their ˈsacred ˈfeasts a ˈsnare.

25 Let their eyes be darkened, that they ˈmay not ˈsee, *
    and give them continual ˈtrembling ˈin their ˈloins.

26 Pour out your indigˈnation upˈon them, *
    and let the fierceness of your ˈanger ˈoverˈtake them.

27 Let their ˈcamp be ˈdesolate, *
    and let there be ˈnone to ˈdwell in their ˈtents.

153

Ray Francis Brown

154

Jonathan Battishill

28 For they persecute him whom 'you have 'stricken *
    and add to the pain of 'those whom 'you have 'pierced.

29 Lay to their charge 'guilt upon 'guilt, *
    and let them not re'ceive your 'vindi'cation.

†30 Let them be wiped out of the 'book of the 'living *
    and not be 'written a'mong the 'righteous.

153 *Ray Francis Brown*

155 *Edmund T. Chipp*

31 As for me, I am af¦flicted and in¦pain; *
   your help, O God, will¦lift me¦up on¦high.

32 I will praise the Name of¦God in¦song; *
   I will pro¦claim his¦greatness with¦thanksgiving.

33 This will please the LORD more than an¦offering of¦oxen, *
   more than¦bullocks with¦horns and¦hoofs.

34 The afflicted shall¦see and be¦glad; *
   you who seek¦God, your¦heart shall¦live.

35 For the LORD¦listens to the¦needy, *
   and his prisoners¦he does¦not de¦spise.

36 Let the heavens and the¦eärth¦praise him, *
   the seas and¦all that¦möves¦in them;

37 For God will save Zion and rebuild the¦cities of¦Judah; *
   they shall live there and¦have it¦in pos¦session.

38 The children of his¦servants will in¦herit it, *
   and those who love his¦Name will¦dwell there¦in.

Psalm 70   *Deus, in adjutorium*

156   *George A. Macfarren*   **157**   *Frederick Burgomaster*

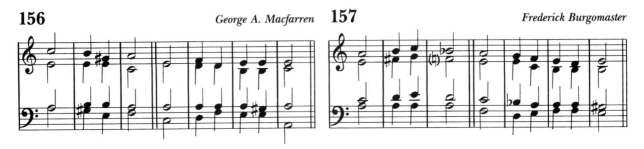

1 Be pleased, O ‖God, to de‖liver me; *
   O ‖LORD, make ‖haste to ‖help me.

2 Let those who seek my life be ashamed
   and alto‖gether dis‖mayed; *
      let those who take pleasure in my misfortune
      draw ‖back and ‖be dis‖graced.

3 Let those who say to me “Aha!” and gloat over me ‖türn ‖back, *
      be‖cause they ‖are a‖shamed.

4 Let all who seek you re‖joice and be ‖glad in you; *
      let those who love your salvation say for ever,
      ‖“Grëat ‖is the ‖LORD!”

5 But as for me, I am ‖poor and ‖needy; *
      come to me ‖speedi‖ly, O ‖God.

6 You are my helper and ‖my de‖liverer; *
      O ‖LÖRD, ‖do not ‖tarry.

Psalm 71   *In te, Domine, speravi*

158   *John Goss*

159   *Ivor Algernon Atkins*

1 In you, O LORD, have I'taken'refuge; *
    let me'never'be a'shamed.

2 In your righteousness, deliver me and'set me'free; *
    incline your'ear to'me and'save me.

3 Be my strong rock, a castle to'keep me'safe; *
    you'are my'crag and my'stronghold.

4 Deliver me, my God, from the'hand of the'wicked, *
    from the clutches of the evil'doer'and the op'pressor.

5 For you are my hope, O'Lörd'GOD, *
    my'confidence since'I was'young.

6 I have been sustained by you ever since I was born;
    from my mother's womb you have'been my'strength; *
    my'praise shall be'always of'you.

7 I have become a'portent to'many; *
    but you are my'refuge'and my'strength.

8 Let my mouth be'full of your'praise *
    and your'glory'all the day'long.

158

John Goss

159

Ivor Algernon Atkins

9 Do not cast me off in my ˈöldˈage; *
     forsake meˈnot when myˈstrēngthˈfails.

10 For my enemies areˈtalking aˈgainst me, *
     and those who lie in wait for myˈlife takeˈcounsel toˈgether.

11 They say, "God has forsaken him;
     goˈafter him andˈseize him; *
       beˈcause there isˈnone who willˈsave."

12 O God,ˈbe notˈfar from me; *
     come quickly toˈhelp me,ˈO myˈGod.

13 Let those who set themselves against me be put to
       shame andˈbe disˈgraced; *
     let those who seek to do me evil beˈcovered withˈscorn and reˈproach.

14 But I shall alwaysˈwait inˈpatience, *
     and shallˈpraise youˈmore andˈmore.

15 My mouth shall recount your mighty acts
     and saving deedsˈall dayˈlong; *
       though I cannotˈknow theˈnumber ofˈthem.

16 I will begin with the mighty works of theˈLördˈGOD; *
     I will recall yourˈrighteousness,ˈyours aˈlone.

146

17 O God, you have taught me since ꞌI was ꞌyoung, *
   and to this day I ꞌtell of your ꞌwonderful ꞌworks.

18 And now that I am old and gray-headed, O God, do ꞌnot for ꞌsake me, *
   till I make known your strength to this generation
   and your power to ꞌall who ꞌare to ꞌcome.

19 Your righteousness, O God, ꞌreaches to the ꞌheavens; *
   you have done great things;
   ꞌwho is like ꞌyou, O ꞌGod?

20 You have showed me great ꞌtroubles and ad ꞌversities, *
   but you will restore my life
   and bring me up again from the deep ꞌplaces ꞌof the ꞌearth.

21 You strengthen me ꞌmore and ꞌmore; *
   — ꞌyou en ꞌfold and ꞌcomfort me,

22 Therefore I will praise you upon the lyre for your
          faithfulness, ꞌO my ꞌGod; *
   I will sing to you with the harp, O ꞌHoly ꞌOne of ꞌIsrael.

23 My lips will sing with ꞌjoy when I ꞌplay to you, *
   and so will my ꞌsoul, which ꞌyou have re ꞌdeemed.

24 My tongue will proclaim your righteousness ꞌall day ꞌlong, *
   for they are ashamed and disgraced who ꞌsought to ꞌdo me ꞌharm.

Psalm 72 *Deus, judicium*

160

Stephen Elvey

161

DESCANT

Walter Galpin Alcock   Descant: John Bertalot

1 Give the King your|justice, O|God, *
    and your|righteousness to the|King's|Son;

2 That he may rule your|people|righteously *
    —|and the|poor with|justice;

3 That the mountains may bring pros|perity to the|people, *
    and the|little|hills bring|righteousness.

4 He shall defend the needy a|mong the|people; *
    he shall rescue the|poor and|crush the op|pressor.

5 He shall live as long as the sun and|moon en|dure, *
    from one gene|ration|to an|other.

6 He shall come down like rain upon the|möwn|field, *
    like|showers that|water the|earth.

†7 In his time shall the|righteous|flourish; *
    there shall be abundance of peace till the|moon shall|be no|more.

148

8 He shall rule from ˈsea to ˈsea, *
  and from the ˈRiver to the ˈends of the ˈearth.

9 His foes shall bow ˈdown beˈfore him, *
  and his ˈenemies ˈlick the ˈdust.

10 The kings of Tarshish and of the ˈisles shall pay ˈtribute, *
  and the kings of Arabia and ˈSaba ˈoffer ˈgifts.

11 All kings shall bow ˈdown beˈfore him, *
  and all the ˈnations ˈdo him ˈservice.

12 For he shall deliver the poor who cries ˈout in disˈtress, *
  and the opˈpressed who ˈhas no ˈhelper.

13 He shall have pity on the ˈlowly and ˈpoor; *
  he shall preˈserve the ˈlives of the ˈneedy.

14 He shall redeem their lives from opˈpression and ˈviolence, *
  and dear shall their ˈblood be ˈin his ˈsight.

15 Long may he live!
  and may there be given to him ˈgold from Aˈrabia; *
    may prayer be made for him always,
    and may they ˈbless him ˈall the day ˈlong.

16 May there be abundance of grain on the earth,
  growing thick ˈeven on the ˈhilltops; *
    may its fruit flourish like Lebanon,
    and its grain like ˈgrass upˈon the ˈearth.

17 May his Name remain for ever,
  and be established as long as the ˈsun enˈdures; *
    may all the nations bless themselves in ˈhim and ˈcall him ˈblessed.

18 Blessèd be the Lord GOD, the ˈGod of ˈIsrael, *
  who aˈlone does ˈwondrous ˈdeeds!

19 And blessèd be his glorious ˈName for ˈever! *
  and may all the earth be filled with his glory.
    ˈAmen. ˈÄˈmen.

Psalm 73   *Quam bonus Israel!*

162   *James Turle*

163   *Joseph Barnby*

1 Truly, God is 'good to 'Israel, *
   to 'those who are 'pure in 'heart.

2 But as for me, my feet had 'nearly 'slipped; *
   I had 'almost 'tripped and 'fallen;

3 Because I 'envied the 'proud *
   and saw the pros'perity 'of the 'wicked:

4 For they 'suffer no 'pain, *
   and their 'bodies are 'sleek and 'sound;

5 In the misfortunes of others they 'have no 'share; *
   they are not af'flicted as 'others 'are;

6 Therefore they wear their 'pride like a 'necklace *
   and wrap their violence a'bout them 'like a 'cloak.

7 Their iniquity comes from 'gröss 'minds, *
   and their hearts over'flow with 'wicked 'thoughts.

8 They scoff and 'speak ma'liciously; *
   out of their 'haughtiness they 'plan op'pression.

150

9 They set their mouths a'gainst the 'heavens, *
   and their evil 'speech runs 'through the 'world.

10 And so the 'people 'turn to them *
   and 'find in 'them no 'fault.

11 They say, '"How should 'God know? *
   is there 'knowledge in the 'Möst 'High?"

12 So then, 'these are the 'wicked; *
   always at 'ease, they in'crease their 'wealth.

13 In vain have I kept my 'heärt 'clean, *
   and 'washed my 'hands in 'innocence.

14 I have been afflicted 'all day 'long, *
   and 'punished 'every 'morning.

15 Had I gone on 'speaking this 'way, *
   I should have betrayed the gene'ration 'of your 'children.

16 When I tried to under'stand these 'things, *
   it 'was too 'hard for 'me;

17 Until I entered the 'sanctuary of 'God *
   and dis'cerned the 'end of the 'wicked.

18 Surely, you set them in 'slippery 'places; *
   you 'cast them 'down in 'ruin.

19 Oh, how suddenly do they 'come to de'struction, *
   come to an 'end, and 'perish from 'terror!

20 Like a dream when one a'wakens, O 'Lord, *
   when you arise you will 'make their 'image 'vanish.

21 When my mind be'came em'bittered, *
   I was sorely 'wounded 'in my 'heart.

22 I was stupid and had 'no under'standing; *
   I was like a brute 'beäst 'in your 'presence.

162

James Turle

163

Joseph Barnby

23 Yet I am'always'with you; *
  you hold me'by my'right'hand.

24 You will'guide me by your'counsel, *
  and'afterwards re'ceive me with'glory.

25 Whom have I in'heaven but'you? *
  and having you I de'sire'nothing upon'earth.

26 Though my flesh and my heart should'waste a'way, *
  God is the strength of my'heart and my'portion for'ever.

27 Truly, those who for'sake you will'perish; *
  you destroy'all who'are un'faithful.

28 But it is good for me to be'near'God; *
  I have made the'Lord'GOD my'refuge.

†29 I will speak of'all your'works *
  in the'gates of the'city of'Zion.

152

Psalm 74   *Ut quid, Deus?*

164   *Joseph Harris*

165   *James Turle*

Setting 1: #164; setting 2: #165–166.

1 O God, why have you utterly |cast us |off? *
    why is your wrath so |hot against the |sheep of your |pasture?

2 Remember your congregation that you purchased |long a|go, *
    the tribe you redeemed to be your inheritance,
    and Mount |Zion |where you |dwell.

3 Turn your steps toward the |endless |ruins; *
    the enemy has laid waste |everything |in your |sanctuary.

4 Your adversaries roared in your |holy |place; *
    they set up their |banners as |tokens of |victory.

5 They were like men coming up with axes to a |grove of |trees; *
    they broke down all your carved |work with |hatchets and |hammers.

6 They set fire to your |holy |place; *
    they defiled the dwelling-place of your Name
    and |razed it |to the |ground.

7 They said to themselves, "Let us destroy them |alto|gether." *
    They burned down all the meeting-places of |Göd |in the |land.

8 There are no signs for us to see;
    there is no |prophet |left; *
    there is not one a|mong us who |knows how |long.

164

Joseph Harris

165

James Turle

9 How long, O God, will the ˈadversary ˈscoff? *
    will the enemy blasˈpheme your ˈName for ˈever?

10 Why do you drawˈback your ˈhand? *
    why is your right hand ˈhidden ˈin your ˈbosom?

11 Yet God is my King from ˈancient ˈtimes, *
    victorious in the ˈmïdst ˈof the ˈearth.

12 You divided the ˈsea by your ˈmight *
    and shattered the heads of the ˈdragons upˈon the ˈwaters;

13 You crushed the ˈheads of Leˈviathan *
    and gave him to the ˈpeople of the ˈdesert for ˈfood.

14 You split open ˈspring and ˈtorrent; *
    you dried up ˈever-ˈflowing ˈrivers.

15 Yours is the day, yours ˈalso the ˈnight; *
    you esˈtablished the ˈmoon and the ˈsun.

16 You fixed all the ˈboundaries of the ˈearth; *
    you ˈmade both ˈsummer and ˈwinter.

17 Remember, O LORD, how the ˈenemy ˈscoffed, *
    how a foolish ˈpeople deˈspised your ˈName.

18 Do not hand over the life of your dove to ˈwild ˈbeasts; *
    never forˈget the ˈlives of your ˈpoor.

154

19 Look up'on your 'covenant; *
  the dark places of the 'earth are 'haunts of 'violence.

20 Let not the oppressed turn a'way a'shamed; *
  let the poor and 'needy 'praise your 'Name.

164

Joseph Harris

166

James Turle

21 Arise, O God, main'tain your 'cause; *
  remember how fools re'vile you 'all day 'long.

22 Forget not the 'clamor of your 'adversaries, *
  the unending tumult of those who 'rise 'up a'gainst you.

Psalm 75 *Confitebimur tibi*

167

Highmore Skeats, Jr.

168

Richard Woodward

1 We give you thanks, O God, we ˈgive you ˈthanks, *
  calling upon your Name and declaring ˈall your ˈwonderful ˈdeeds.

2 "I will appoint a ˈtime," says ˈGod; *
  — ˈ"I will ˈjudge with ˈequity.

3 Though the earth and all its in ˈhabitants are ˈquaking, *
  I will ˈmake its ˈpillars ˈfast.

4 I will say to the boasters, ˈ ˈ'Boast no ˈmore,' *
  and to the wicked, ˈ ˈ'Do not ˈtoss your ˈhorns;

5 Do not toss your ˈhorns so ˈhigh, *
  nor ˈspeak with a ˈprŏud ˈneck.' "

6 For judgment is neither from the ˈeast nor from the ˈwest, *
  nor yet from the ˈwilderness ˈor the ˈmountains.

7 It is⟨God who⟨judges; *

he puts down⟨one and⟨lifts up an⟨other.

8 For in the LORD's hand there is a cup,

full of spiced and foaming wine, which he⟨poürs⟨out, *

and all the wicked of the earth shall⟨drink and⟨drain the⟨dregs.

9 But I will re⟨joice for⟨ever; *

I will sing⟨praises to the⟨God of⟨Jacob.

10 He shall break off all the⟨horns of the⟨wicked; *

but the horns of the⟨righteous shall⟨be ex⟨alted.

Psalm 76 *Notus in Judaea*

169

John Naylor

170

C. Hylton Stewart

1 In Judah is ˈGödˈknown; *
    hisˈName isˈgreat inˈIsrael.

2 AtˈSalem is hisˈtabernacle, *
    and hisˈdwellingˈis inˈZion.

3 There he broke theˈflashingˈarrows, *
    the shield, theˈsword, and theˈweapons ofˈbattle.

4 How ˈglorious you ˈare! *

more splendid than the ˈeverˈlasting ˈmountains!

5 The strong of heart have been despoiled;
they ˈsink into ˈsleep; *

none of the ˈwarriors can ˈlift a ˈhand.

6 At your rebuke, O ˈGod of ˈJacob, *

both ˈhorse and ˈrider lie ˈstunned.

7 What ˈterror you in ˈspire! *

who can stand be ˈfore you when ˈyou are ˈangry?

8 From heaven you pro ˈnoünced ˈjudgment; *

the ˈearth was a ˈfraid and was ˈstill;

9 When God rose ˈup to ˈjudgment *

and to save ˈall the op ˈpressed of the ˈearth.

10 Truly, wrathful Edom will ˈgive you ˈthanks, *

and the remnant of ˈHamath will ˈkeep your ˈfeasts.

11 Make a vow to the LORD your ˈGod and ˈkeep it; *

let all around him bring gifts to him who is ˈworthy ˈto be ˈfeared.

12 He breaks the ˈspirit of ˈprinces, *

and strikes ˈterror in the ˈkings of the ˈearth.

159

Psalm 77   *Voce mea ad Dominum*

171   *Ray Francis Brown*

172   *Douglas Major*

1 I will cry a'loud to 'God; *
    I will cry a'loud, and 'he will 'hear me.

2 In the day of my trouble I 'sought the 'Lord; *
    my hands were stretched out by night and did not tire;
    'I re'fused to be 'comforted.

3 I think of God, 'I am 'restless, *
    I ponder, 'and my 'spirit 'faints.

4 You will not let my 'eyelids 'close; *
    I am 'troubled and I 'cannot 'speak.

5 I consider the 'days of 'old; *
    I re'member the 'years long 'past;

6 I commune with my 'heart in the 'night; *
    I 'ponder and 'search my 'mind.

7 Will the Lord cast me 'off for 'ever? *
    Will he 'no more 'show his 'favor?

8 Has his loving-kindness come to an 'end for 'ever? *
    has his promise 'failed for 'ever'more?

†9 Has God for'gotten to be 'gracious? *
    has he, in his 'anger, with'held his com'passion?

10 And I said, "My'grief is'this: *
    the right hand of the Most'High has'lost its'power."

11 I will remember the'works of the'LORD, *
    and call to mind your'wonders of'öld'time.

†12 I will meditate on'all your'acts *
    and'ponder your'mighty'deeds.

13 Your way, O'God, is'holy; *
    who is so'great a'god as'our God?

14 You are the God who'wörks'wonders *
    and have declared your'power a'mong the'peoples.

15 By your strength you have re'deemed your'people, *
    the'children of'Jacob and'Joseph.

16 The waters saw you, O God;
    the waters'saw you and'trembled; *
    the'very'depths were'shaken.

17 The clouds poured out water;
    the'skïes'thundered; *
    your'arrows flashed'to and'fro;

18 The sound of your thunder was in the whirlwind;
    your lightnings lit'up the'world; *
    the'eärth'trembled and'shook.

19 Your way was in the sea,
    and your paths in the'grëat'waters, *
    yet your'footsteps'were not'seen.

20 You led your'people like a'flock *
    by the'hand of'Moses and'Aaron.

Psalm 78: Part 1 *Attendite, popule*

173 *C. Hylton Stewart*

176 *John Goss*

Setting 1: #173–175; setting 2: #176–178.

1 Hear my teaching, ˈO myˈpeople; *
   incline yourˈears to theˈwords of myˈmouth.

2 I will open myˈmouth in aˈparable; *
   I will declare theˈmysteries ofˈancientˈtimes.

3 That which we have heard and known,
   and what ourˈforefathers haveˈtold us, *
   we will notˈhïdeˈfrom theirˈchildren.

4 We will recount to generations to come
   the praiseworthy deeds and theˈpower of theˈLORD, *
   and the wonderfulˈwörksˈhe hasˈdone.

5 He gave his decrees to Jacob
   and established aˈlaw forˈIsrael, *
   which he comˈmanded them toˈteach theirˈchildren;

6 That the generations to come might know,
   and the childrenˈyet unˈborn; *
   that they in their turn mightˈtell itˈto theirˈchildren;

162

7 So that they might put their ˈtrust in ˈGod, *
    and not forget the deeds of God,
        but ˈkëep ˈhis comˈmandments;

8 And not be like their forefathers,
    a stubborn and reˈbellious geneˈration, *
        a generation whose heart was not steadfast,
        and whose ˈspirit was not ˈfaithful to ˈGod.

174

Thomas Jackson

177

John Goss

9 The people of Ephraim, ˈarmed with the ˈbow, *
    turned ˈback in the ˈday of ˈbattle;

10 They did not keep the ˈcovenant of ˈGod, *
    and reˈfused to ˈwalk in his ˈlaw;

11 They forˈgot what he had ˈdone, *
    and the ˈwonders ˈhe had ˈshown them.

12 He worked marvels in the ˈsight of their ˈforefathers, *
    in the land of ˈEgypt, in the ˈfield of ˈZoan.

13 He split open the sea and ˈlet them pass ˈthrough; *
    he made the ˈwaters stand ˈup like ˈwalls.

14 He led them with a ˈcloud by ˈday, *
    and all the night ˈthrough with a ˈglow of ˈfire.

174

Thomas Jackson

177

John Goss

15 He split the hard'rocks in the'wilderness *
  and gave them drink as'from the'grëat'deep.

16 He brought streams'out of the'cliff, *
  and the'waters gushed'out like'rivers.

†17 But they went on'sinning a'gainst him, *
  rebelling in the desert a'gainst the'Möst'High.

175 *Ray Francis Brown*

178 *Robert Cooke*

18 They tested ˈGod in their ˈhearts, *
    deˈmanding ˈfood for their ˈcraving.

19 They railed against ˈGod and ˈsaid, *
    "Can God set a ˈtable ˈin the ˈwilderness?

20 True, he struck the rock, the waters gushed out, and the ˈgullies overˈflowed; *
    but is he able to give bread
    or to provide ˈmëat ˈfor his ˈpeople?"

21 When the LORD heard this, he was ˈfull of ˈwrath; *
    a fire was kindled against Jacob,
    and his anger ˈmounted aˈgaïnst ˈIsrael;

22 For they had no ˈfaith in ˈGod, *
    nor did they put their ˈtrust in his ˈsaving ˈpower.

23 So he commanded the ˈclouds aˈbove *
    and ˈopened the ˈdoors of ˈheaven.

24 He rained down manna upˈon them to ˈeat *
    and ˈgave them ˈgrain from ˈheaven.

25 So mortals ate the ˈbread of ˈangels; *
    he proˈvided for them ˈfood eˈnough.

175

Ray Francis Brown

178

Robert Cooke

26 He caused the east wind to ' blow in the ' heavens *
   and led out the ' south wind ' by his ' might.

27 He rained down flesh up ' on them like ' dust *
   and wingèd ' birds like the ' sand of the ' sea.

28 He let it fall in the ' midst of their ' camp *
   and ' round a ' bout their ' dwellings.

29 So they ate and were ' wëll ' filled, *
   for he ' gave them ' what they ' craved.

173   *C. Hylton Stewart*

176   *John Goss*

30 But they did not'stop their'craving, *
   though the'food was'still in their'mouths.

31 So God's anger'mounted a'gainst them; *
   he slew their strongest men
   and laid'low the'youth of'Israel.

32 In spite of all this, they'went on'sinning *
   and had no'faith in his'wonderful'works.

33 So he brought their days to an'end like a'breath *
   and their'years in'sudden'terror.

34 Whenever he slew them,'they would'seek him, *
   and repent, and'diligently'search for'God.

35 They would remember that'God was their'rock, *
   and the Most'High God'their re'deemer.

36 But they flattered him'with their'mouths *
   and'lied to him'with their'tongues.

37 Their heart was not'steadfast'toward him, *
   and they were not'faithful'to his'covenant.

173   *C. Hylton Stewart*

176   *John Goss*

38 But he was so merciful that he forgave their sins
   and ˈdid not desˈtroy them; *

      many times he held back his anger
      and did not perˈmit hisˈwrath to beˈroused.

39 For he remembered thatˈthey were butˈflesh, *
      a breath that goesˈforth andˈdoes not reˈturn.

Psalm 78: Part 2   *Quoties exacerbaverunt*

174   *Thomas Jackson*

177   *John Goss*

40 How often the people disobeyed him ⌐in the⌐wilderness *
     and of⌐fended him ⌐in the⌐desert!

41 Again and again they⌐tempted⌐God *
     and provoked the⌐Holy⌐One of⌐Israel.

42 They did not re⌐member his⌐power *
     in the day when he⌐ransomed them⌐from the⌐enemy;

43 How he wrought his⌐signs in⌐Egypt *
     and his⌐omens in the⌐field of⌐Zoan.

44 He turned their⌐rivers into⌐blood, *
     so that they⌐could not⌐drink of their⌐streams.

45 He sent swarms of flies among them, which⌐ate them⌐up, *
     and⌐frögs,⌐which de⌐stroyed them.

46 He gave their⌐crops to the⌐caterpillar, *
     the fruit of their⌐töil⌐to the⌐locust.

47 He killed their⌐vines with⌐hail *
     —⌐and their⌐sycamores with⌐frost.

169

174

Thomas Jackson

177

John Goss

48 He delivered their ˈcattle to ˈhailstones *
   and their ˈlivestock to ˈhöt ˈthunderbolts.

49 He poured out upon them his ˈblazing ˈanger: *
   fury, indignation, and distress,
   a ˈtroop of deˈstroying ˈangels.

50 He gave full rein to his anger;
   he did not spare their ˈsouls from ˈdeath; *
   but deˈlivered their ˈlives to the ˈplague.

51 He struck down all the ˈfirstborn of ˈEgypt, *
   the flower of ˈmanhood in the ˈdwellings of ˈHam.

52 He led out his ˈpeople like ˈsheep *
   and guided them in the ˈwilderness ˈlike a ˈflock.

53 He led them to safety, and they were ˈnot aˈfraid; *
   but the sea ˈoverˈwhelmed their ˈenemies.

54 He brought them to his ˈholy ˈland, *
   the mountain his ˈrïght ˈhand had ˈwon.

55 He drove out the Canaanites before them
   and apportioned an inheritance to ˈthem by ˈlot; *
   he made the tribes of ˈIsrael to ˈdwell in their ˈtents.

175

Ray Francis Brown

178

Robert Cooke

56 But they tested the Most High 'God, and de'fied him, *
   and 'did not 'keep his com'mandments.

57 They turned away and were dis'loyal like their 'fathers; *
   they were undependable 'like a 'warped 'bow.

†58 They grieved him 'with their 'hill-altars *
   and provoked his dis'pleasure 'with their 'idols.

59 When God heard 'this, he was 'angry *
   and 'utterly re'jected 'Israel.

60 He forsook the 'shrine at 'Shiloh, *
   the tabernacle where he had 'lived a'mong his 'people.

61 He delivered the ark 'into cap'tivity, *
   his glory 'into the 'adversary's 'hand.

62 He gave his 'people to the 'sword *
   and was 'angered a'gainst his in'heritance.

63 The fire consumed their 'young 'men; *
   there were no 'wedding songs 'for their 'maidens.

64 Their priests 'fell by the 'sword, *
   and their widows 'made no 'lamen'tation.

173

C. Hylton Stewart

176

John Goss

65 Then the LORD woke as┐though from┐sleep, *
   like a┐warrior re┐freshed with┐wine.

66 He struck his enemies┐on the┐backside *
   and┐put them to per┐petual┐shame.

67 He rejected the┐tent of┐Joseph *
   and did not┐choose the┐tribe of┐Ephraim;

68 He chose instead the┐tribe of┐Judah *
   and Mount┐Zion,┐which he┐loved.

69 He built his sanctuary like the┐heights of┐heaven, *
   like the┐earth which he┐founded for┐ever.

70 He chose┐David his┐servant, *
   and┐took him a┐way from the┐sheepfolds.

71 He brought him from┐following the┐ewes, *
   to be a shepherd over Jacob his people
   and over┐Israel┐his in┐heritance.

72 So he shepherded them with a faithful and┐trüe┐heart *
   and guided them with the┐skillfulness┐of his┐hands.

Psalm 79 *Deus, venerunt*

179

Richard Clark

180

David Hurd

1 O God, the heathen have come into your inheritance;
   they have profaned your ˈholy ˈtemple; *
      they have made Jeˈrusalem a ˈheap of ˈrubble.

2 They have given the bodies of your servants as food for
                  the ˈbirds of the ˈair, *
      and the flesh of your faithful ones ˈto the ˈbeasts of the ˈfield.

3 They have shed their blood like water on every ˈside of Jeˈrusalem, *
      and ˈthere was ˈno one to ˈbury them.

4 We have become a reˈproach to our ˈneighbors, *
      an object of scorn and deˈrision to ˈthose aˈround us.

5 How long will you be ˈangry, O ˈLORD? *
      will your fury ˈblaze like ˈfire for ˈever?

6 Pour out your wrath upon the heathen who ˈhave not ˈknown you *
      and upon the kingdoms that have not ˈcalled upˈon your ˈName.

7 For they have deˈvoüred ˈJacob *
      and ˈmade his ˈdwelling a ˈruin.

8 Remember not our past sins;
   let your compassion be ˈswift to ˈmeet us; *
      for ˈwe have been ˈbrought very ˈlow.

173

179

Richard Clark

180

David Hurd

9 Help us, O God our Savior, for the 'glory of your 'Name; *
   deliver us and forgive us our 'sins, for your 'Name's 'sake.

10 Why should the heathen say, '"Where is their 'God?" *
   Let it be known among the heathen and in our sight
   that you avenge the 'shedding of your 'servants' 'blood.

11 Let the sorrowful sighing of the prisoners 'come be'fore you, *
   and by your great might spare 'those who are con'demned to 'die.

12 May the revilings with which they re'viled you, O 'Lord, *
   return 'seven-fold 'into their 'bosoms.

†13 For we are your people and the 'sheep of your 'pasture; *
   we will give you thanks for ever
   and show forth your 'praise from 'age to 'age.

Psalm 80 *Qui regis Israel*

181

Jonathan Battishill

182

Henry Walford Davies

Setting 1: #181; setting 2: #182–183

1 Hear, O Shepherd of Israel, leading ⌐Joseph like a⌐'flock; *
   shine forth, you that are en'throned up'on the'cherubim.

2 In the presence of Ephraim,'⌐Benjamin, and ⌐Ma'nasseh, *
   stir up your'strength and'come to'help us.

†3 Restore us, O'God of'hosts; *
   show the light of your'⌐countenance, and'⌐we shall be'saved.

4 O LORD'God of'hosts, *
   how long will ⌐you be angered
   de'spite the'⌐prayers of your'people?

5 You have fed them with the'bread of'tears; *
   you have given them'bowls of'tears to'drink.

6 You have made us the de'⌐rision of our'⌐neighbors, *
   and our'⌐enemies'⌐laugh us to'scorn.

7 Restore us, O'God of'hosts; *
   show the light of your'⌐countenance, and'⌐we shall be'saved.

175

Jonathan Battishill

183

Henry Walford Davies

8 You have brought a 'vine out of 'Egypt; *
   you cast 'out the 'nations and 'planted it.

9 You pre 'pared the 'ground for it; *
   it took 'root and 'filled the 'land.

10 The mountains were 'covered by its 'shadow *
   and the towering 'cedar trees 'by its 'boughs.

11 You stretched out its 'tendrils to the 'Sea *
   and its 'branches 'to the 'River.

12 Why have you broken 'down its 'wall, *
   so that all who pass 'by pluck 'off its 'grapes?

13 The wild boar of the 'forest has 'ravaged it, *
   and the beasts of the 'field have 'grazed up 'on it.

†14 Turn now, O God of hosts, look down from heaven;
   behold and 'tend this 'vine; *
   preserve what 'your right 'hand has 'planted.

15 They burn it with 'fire like 'rubbish; *
   at the rebuke of your 'countenance 'let them 'perish.

16 Let your hand be upon the 'man of your 'right hand, *
   the son of man you have 'made so 'strong for your 'self.

181 *Jonathan Battishill*

182 *Henry Walford Davies*

17 And so will we never ¦ turn a ¦ way from you; *
  give us life, that we may ¦ call up ¦ on your ¦ Name.

18 Restore us, O LORD ¦ God of ¦ hosts; *
  show the light of your ¦ countenance, and ¦ we shall be ¦ saved.

Psalm 81   *Exultate Deo*

184   *Robert Prescott Stewart*

185   *George Elvey*

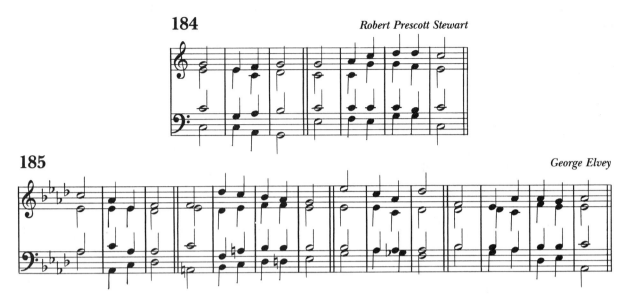

1 Sing with joy to ˈGod our ˈstrength *
  and raise a loud ˈshout to the ˈGod of ˈJacob.

2 Raise a song and ˈsound the ˈtimbrel, *
  the ˈmerry ˈharp, and the ˈlyre.

3 Blow the ram's-horn at the ˈnëw ˈmoon, *
  and at the full ˈmoon, the ˈday of our ˈfeast.

4 For this is a ˈstatute for ˈIsrael, *
  a ˈlaw of the ˈGod of ˈJacob.

5 He laid it as a solemn ˈcharge upon ˈJoseph, *
  when he came ˈout of the ˈland of ˈEgypt.

6 I heard an unfamiliar ˈvoïce ˈsaying, *
  "I eased his shoulder from the burden;
  his hands were set ˈfree from ˈbearing the ˈload."

7 You called on me in ˈtrouble, and I ˈsaved you; *
  I answered you from the secret place of thunder
  and tested ˈyou at the ˈwaters of ˈMeribah.

8 Hear, O my people, and ˈI will ad ˈmonish you: *
  O Israel, if you ˈwould but ˈlisten to ˈme!

178

9 There shall be no strange 'god a'mong you; *
   you shall not 'worship a 'foreign 'god.

10 I am the LORD your God,
   who brought you out of the land of 'Egypt and 'said, *
      "Open your mouth 'wide, and 'I will 'fill it."

11 And yet my people did not 'hear my 'voice, *
   and 'Israel would 'not o'bey me.

12 So I gave them over to the 'stubbornness of their 'hearts, *
   to 'follow their 'own de'vices.

13 Oh, that my 'people would 'listen to me! *
   that 'Israel would 'walk in my 'ways!

14 I should soon sub'due their 'enemies *
   and turn my 'hand a'gainst their 'foes.

15 Those who hate the LORD would 'cringe be'fore him, *
   and their 'punishment would 'last for 'ever.

16 But Israel would I feed with the 'finest 'wheat *
   and satisfy him with 'honey 'from the 'rock.

Psalm 82 *Deus stetit*

186 C. Hylton Stewart **187** David Hurd

1 God takes his stand in the 'council of 'heaven; *
   he gives 'judgment in the 'midst of the 'gods:

2 "How long will you 'judge un'justly, *
   and show 'favor 'to the 'wicked?

3 Save the 'weak and the 'orphan; *
   de'fend the 'humble and 'needy;

4 Rescue the 'weak and the 'poor; *
   deliver them from the 'power 'of the 'wicked.

5 They do not know, neither do they understand;
   they go a'bout in 'darkness; *
   all the foun'dations of the 'earth are 'shaken.

6 Now I say to you, ' 'You are 'gods, *
   and all of you 'children of the 'Möst 'High;

7 Nevertheless, you shall 'die like 'mortals, *
   and 'fall like 'any 'prince.' "

8 Arise, O God, and 'rule the 'earth, *
   for you shall take all 'nations 'for your 'own.

Psalm 83   *Deus, quis similis?*

188   *William Best*

189   *Joseph Harris*

1 O God, do'not be'silent; *
     do not keep still nor'hold your'peace, O'God;

2 For your enemies'are in'tumult, *
     and those who hate you have'lifted'up their'heads.

3 They take secret counsel a'gainst your'people *
     and plot against'those whom'you pro'tect.

4 They have said, "Come, let us wipe them out from
                 a'mong the'nations; *
     let the name of'Israel be re'membered no'more."

5 They have con'spired to'gether; *
     they have'made an al'liance a'gainst you:

6 The tents of'Edom and the'Ishmaelites; *
     the'Moabites'and the'Hagarenes;

7 Gebal, and'Ammon, and'Amalek; *
     the Philistines and'those who'dwell in'Tyre.

8 The Assyrians'also have'joined them, *
     and have come to'help the'people of'Lot.

188

William Best

189

Joseph Harris

9 Do to them as you ' did to ' Midian, *
    to Sisera, and to ' Jabin at the ' river of ' Kishon:

10 They were de ' stroyed at ' Endor; *
    they became like ' dung up ' on the ' ground.

11 Make their leaders like ' Oreb and ' Zeëb, *
    and all their com ' manders like ' Zebah and Zal ' munna,

12 Who said, "Let us ' take for our ' selves *
    the fields of ' God as ' our pos ' session."

13 O my God, make them like ' whirling ' dust *
    and like ' chaff be ' fore the ' wind;

14 Like fire that burns ' down a ' forest, *
    like the ' flame that sets ' mountains a ' blaze.

15 Drive them ' with your ' tempest *
    and ' terrify them ' with your ' storm;

16 Cover their faces with ' shame, O ' LORD, *
    that ' they may ' seek your ' Name.

17 Let them be disgraced and ' terrified for ' ever; *
    let them be ' put to con ' fusion and ' perish.

18 Let them know that you, whose ' Name is ' YAHWEH, *
    you alone are the Most ' High over ' all the ' earth.

Psalm 84   *Quam dilecta!*

190   *Edward John Hopkins*

191   *Charles Hubert Hastings Parry*

1 How dear to me is your dwelling, O'LORD of'hosts! *
    My soul has a desire and longing for the courts of the LORD;
    my heart and my flesh re'joice in the'living'God.

2 The sparrow has found her a house
    and the swallow a nest where she may'lay her'young; *
        by the side of your altars, O LORD of hosts,
        my'King'and my'God.

3 Happy are they who'dwell in your'house! *
    they will'always be'praising'you.

4 Happy are the people whose'strength is in'you! *
    whose hearts are'set on the'pilgrims''way.

5 Those who go through the desolate valley will find
            it a'place of'springs, *
    for the early rains have'covered it with'pools of'water.

6 They will climb from'height to'height, *
    and the God of gods will re'veal him'self in'Zion.

7 LORD God of hosts,'hear my'prayer; *
    —'hearken, O'God of'Jacob.

8 Behold our de'fender, O'God; *
    and look upon the'face of'your A'nointed.

183

190

Edward John Hopkins

191

Charles Hubert Hastings Parry

9 For one day in your courts is better than a thousand in my ˈownˈroom, *
  and to stand at the threshold of the house of my God
  than toˈdwell in theˈtents of theˈwicked.

10 For the LORD God is bothˈsun andˈshield; *
  —ˈhe will giveˈgrace andˈglory;

11 No good thing will theˈLORD withˈhold *
  fromˈthose whoˈwalk with inˈtegrity.

12 OˈLORD ofˈhosts, *
  happy are they whoˈput theirˈtrust inˈyou!

Psalm 85   *Benedixisti, Domine*

192   *Samuel Sebastian Wesley*

193   *John Joubert*

1 You have been gracious to your 'land, O 'LORD, *
   you have re'stored the good 'fortune of 'Jacob.

2 You have forgiven the in'iquity of your 'people *
   and 'blotted out 'all their 'sins.

†3 You have withdrawn 'all your 'fury *
   and turned yourself from your 'wrathful 'indig'nation.

4 Restore us then, O 'God our 'Savior; *
   — 'let your 'anger de'part from us.

5 Will you be dis'pleased with us for 'ever? *
   will you prolong your 'anger from 'age to 'age?

6 Will you not give us 'life a'gain, *
   that your 'people may re'joice in 'you?

7 Show us your 'mercy, O 'LORD, *
   and 'grant us 'your sal'vation.

8 I will listen to what the LORD 'God is 'saying, *
   for he is speaking peace to his faithful people
   and to 'those who 'turn their 'hearts to him.

192 *Samuel Sebastian Wesley*

193 *John Joubert*

9 Truly, his salvation is very near to ˈthose who ˈfear him, *
  that his ˈglory may ˈdwell in our ˈland.

10 Mercy and truth have ˈmet to ˈgether; *
  righteousness and ˈpeace have ˈkissed each ˈother.

11 Truth shall spring ˈup from the ˈearth, *
  and righteousness shall ˈlöok ˈdown from ˈheaven.

12 The LORD will indeed ˈgrant prosˈperity, *
  and our ˈland will ˈyield its ˈincrease.

13 Righteousness shall ˈgo beˈfore him, *
  and peace shall be a ˈpathway ˈfor his ˈfeet.

Psalm 86   *Inclina, Domine*

194

William Crotch

195

John Foster

1 Bow down your ear, O'LORD, and 'answer me, *
   for 'I am 'poor and in 'misery.

2 Keep watch over my life, for 'I am 'faithful; *
   save your 'servant who 'puts his 'trust in you.

3 Be merciful to me, O LORD, for 'you are my 'God; *
   I call up 'on you 'all the day 'long.

4 Gladden the 'soul of your 'servant, *
   for to you, O 'LORD, I 'lift up my 'soul.

5 For you, O LORD, are 'good and for 'giving, *
   and great is your love toward 'all who 'call up 'on you.

6 Give ear, O 'LORD, to my 'prayer, *
   and attend to the 'voice of my 'suppli 'cations.

7 In the time of my trouble I will 'call upon 'you, *
   for 'you will 'answer 'me.

8 Among the gods there is none like 'you, O 'LORD, *
   nor 'anything 'like your 'works.

187

194

195

9 All nations you have made will come and worship'you, O'LORD, *
   and'glori'fy your'Name.

10 For you are great;
   you do'wondrous'things; *
    and'you a'lone are'God.

11 Teach me your way, O LORD,
   and I will'walk in your'truth; *
    knit my heart to you that'I may'fear your'Name.

12 I will thank you, O LORD my God, with'all my'heart, *
   and glorify your'Name for'ever'more.

†13 For great is your'löve'toward me; *
   you have de'livered me from the'nethermost'Pit.

14 The arrogant rise up against me, O God,
   and a band of violent men'seeks my'life; *
    they have not set'you be'fore their'eyes.

15 But you, O LORD, are gracious and'full of com'passion, *
   slow to anger, and'full of'kindness and'truth.

16 Turn to me and haveˈmercy upˈon me; *
　　give your strength to your servant;
　　andˈsave theˈchild of yourˈhandmaid.

17 Show me a sign of your favor,
　　so that those who hate me may see it andˈbe aˈshamed; *
　　because you, OˈLORD, haveˈhelped me andˈcomforted me.

Psalm 87 *Fundamenta ejus*

196　　　　　　　　　　　　　　　*Edwin George Monk*

197　　　　　　　　　　　　　　　*John Goss*

1 On the holy mountain stands theˈcity he hasˈfounded; *
　　the LORD loves the gates of Zion
　　more thanˈall theˈdwellings ofˈJacob.

2 Glorious things areˈspoken ofˈyou, *
　　Oˈcityˈof ourˈGod.

3 I count Egypt and Babylon amongˈthose whoˈknow me; *
　　behold Philistia, Tyre, and Ethiopia:
　　inˈZionˈwere theyˈborn.

4 Of Zion it shall be said,ˈ"Everyone wasˈborn in her, *
　　and the MostˈHigh himˈself shall susˈtain her."

5 The LORD will record as he enˈrolls theˈpeoples, *
　　—ˈ"Thëseˈalso wereˈborn there."

6 The singers and theˈdancers willˈsay, *
　　"Allˈmy freshˈsprings are inˈyou."

189

Psalm 88   *Domine, Deus*

198

Cambridge Chant

199

Derrick Cantrell

1 O LORD, my ' God, my ' Savior, *
   by ' day and ' night I ' cry to you.

2 Let my prayer enter ' into your ' presence; *
   incline your ' ear to my ' lamen ' tation.

3 For I am ' full of ' trouble; *
   my life is ' at the ' brink of the ' grave.

4 I am counted among those who go ' down to the ' Pit; *
   I have become like ' one who ' has no ' strength;

5 Lost a ' mong the ' dead, *
   like the ' slain who ' lie in the ' grave,

6 Whom you re ' member no ' more, *
   for ' they are cut ' off from your ' hand.

7 You have laid me in the ' depths of the ' Pit, *
   in dark ' places, and ' in the a ' byss.

8 Your anger weighs up ' on me ' heavily, *
   and all your great ' waves ' over ' whelm me.

190

9 You have put my friends far from me;
  you have made me to'be ab'horred by them; *
    I am in'prison and'cannot get'free.

10 My sight has failed me be'cause of'trouble; *
   LORD, I have called upon you daily;
    'I have stretched'out my'hands to you.

11 Do you work'wonders for the'dead? *
   will those who have died stand'up and'give you'thanks?

12 Will your loving-kindness be de'clared in the'grave? *
   your'faithfulness in the'land of de'struction?

†13 Will your wonders be'known in the'dark? *
   or your righteousness in the'country where'all is for'gotten?

14 But as for me, O LORD, I cry to'you for'help; *
   in the morning my'präyer'comes be'fore you.

15 LORD,'why have you re'jected me? *
   why have you'hidden your'face from'me?

16 Ever since my youth, I have been wretched and at the'point of'death; *
   I have borne your'terrors with a'troubled'mind.

17 Your blazing anger has'swëpt'over me; *
   your'terrors'have de'stroyed me;

18 They surround me all day'long like a'flood; *
   they en'compass me on'every'side.

19 My friend and my neighbor you have'put a'way from me, *
   and'darkness is my'only com'panion.

Psalm 89: Part 1 *Misericordias Domini*

200

John Goss

202

Edward John Hopkins

Setting 1: #200–201; setting 2: #202–205.

1 Your love, O LORD, for‖ever will I‖sing; *
   from age to age my‖mouth will pro‖claim your‖faithfulness.

2 For I am persuaded that your love is es‖tablished for‖ever; *
   you have set your faithfulness‖firmly‖in the‖heavens.

3 "I have made a‖covenant with my‖chosen one; *
   I have sworn an‖oath to‖David my‖servant:

4 'I will establish your‖line for‖ever, *
   and preserve your‖throne for‖all gene‖rations.'"

5 The heavens bear witness to your‖wonders, O‖LORD, *
   and to your faithfulness in the as‖sembly‖of the‖holy ones;

6 For who in the skies can be com‖pared to the‖LORD? *
   who is like the‖LORD a‖mong the‖gods?

7 God is much to be feared in the‖council of the‖holy ones, *
   great and terrible to‖all those‖round a‖bout him.

8 Who is like you, LORD‖God of‖hosts? *
   O mighty LORD, your‖faithfulness is‖all a‖round you.

9 You rule the ⌐raging of the⌐sea *
    and still the⌐surging⌐of its⌐waves.

10 You have crushed Rahab of the deep with a⌐deadly⌐wound; *
    you have scattered your enemies⌐with your⌐mighty⌐arm.

11 Yours are the heavens; the earth⌐also is⌐yours; *
    you laid the foundations of the⌐world and⌐all that is⌐in it.

12 You have made the⌐north and the⌐south; *
    Tabor and⌐Hermon re⌐joice in your⌐Name.

13 You have a⌐mighty⌐arm; *
    strong is your⌐hand and⌐high is your⌐right hand.

14 Righteousness and justice are the foun⌐dations of your⌐throne; *
    love and truth⌐go be⌐fore your⌐face.

15 Happy are the people who know the⌐festal⌐shout! *
    they walk, O⌐Lord, in the⌐light of your⌐presence.

16 They rejoice⌐daily in your⌐Name; *
    they are⌐jubilant⌐in your⌐righteousness.

17 For you are the⌐glory of their⌐strength, *
    and by your⌐favor our⌐might is ex⌐alted.

18 Truly, the⌐Lord is our⌐ruler; *
    the Holy One of⌐Israel⌐is our⌐King.

201

James Turle

203

John Goss

Psalm 89: Part 2 *Tunc locutus es*

201
James Turle

203
John Goss

19 You spoke once in a vision and said to your ˈfaithful ˈpeople: *
    "I have set the crown upon a warrior
    and have exalted one ˈchosen ˈout of the ˈpeople.

20 I have found ˈDavid my ˈservant; *
    with my holy ˈoil have ˈI a ˈnointed him.

21 My hand will ˈhold him ˈfast *
    and my ˈarm will ˈmake him ˈstrong.

22 No ˈenemy shall de ˈceive him, *
    nor any ˈwicked man ˈbring him ˈdown.

23 I will crush his ˈfoes be ˈfore him *
    and ˈstrike down ˈthose who ˈhate him.

24 My faithfulness and ˈlove shall ˈbe with him, *
    and he shall be vic ˈtorious ˈthrough my ˈName.

25 I shall make his do ˈminion ex ˈtend *
    from the ˈGreat Sea ˈto the ˈRiver.

26 He will say to me, ˈ'You are my ˈFather, *
    my God, and the ˈrock of ˈmy sal ˈvation.'

27 I will ˈmake him my ˈfirstborn *
    and ˈhigher than the ˈkings of the ˈearth.

28 I will keep my love for ˈhim for ˈever, *
    and my ˈcovenant will ˈständ ˈfirm for him.

†29 I will establish his ˈline for ˈever *
    and his ˈthrone as the ˈdays of ˈheaven."

30 "If his children forˈsake my ˈlaw, *
    and do not walk acˈcording ˈto my ˈjudgments;

31 If they ˈbreak my ˈstatutes *
    and ˈdo not ˈkeep my comˈmandments;

32 I will punish their transˈgressions with a ˈrod *
    and their inˈiquities ˈwith the ˈlash;

33 But I will not take my ˈlove from ˈhim, *
    nor let my ˈfaithfulness ˈpröve ˈfalse.

34 I will not ˈbreak my ˈcovenant, *
    nor change what has ˈgöne ˈout of my ˈlips.

35 Once for all I have ˈsworn by my ˈholiness: *
    'I ˈwill not ˈlie to ˈDavid.

36 His line shall enˈdure for ˈever *
    and his ˈthrone as the ˈsun beˈfore me;

37 It shall stand fast for everˈmore like the ˈmoon, *
    the abiding ˈwitness ˈin the ˈsky.'"

Tune change

195

201

James Turle

204

Edward John Hopkins

38 But you have cast off and re'jected your a'nointed; *
  you'have be'come en'raged at him.

39 You have broken your covenant'with your'servant, *
  defiled his crown, and'hurled it'to the'ground.

40 You have breached'all his'walls *
  and'laid his'strongholds in'ruins.

41 All who pass'by de'spoil him; *
  he has become the'scörn'of his'neighbors.

42 You have exalted the right'hand of his'foes *
  and made'all his'enemies re'joice.

43 You have turned back the'edge of his'sword *
  and'have not sus'tained him in'battle.

44 You have put an'end to his'splendor *
  and'cast his'throne to the'ground.

45 You have cut short the'days of his'youth *
  and have'covered'him with'shame.

46 How long will you hide yourself, O LORD?
   will you ˈhide yourself for ˈever? *
     how long will your ˈanger ˈburn like ˈfire?

47 Remember, LORD, how ˈshört ˈlife is, *
     how ˈfrail you have ˈmade all ˈflesh.

48 Who can live and ˈnot see ˈdeath? *
     who can save himself from the ˈpower ˈof the ˈgrave?

49 Where, Lord, are your loving ˈkindnesses of ˈold, *
     which you promised ˈDavid ˈin your ˈfaithfulness?

50 Remember, Lord, how your ˈservant is ˈmocked, *
     how I carry in my bosom the ˈtaunts of ˈmany ˈpeoples,

51 The taunts your enemies have ˈhurled, O ˈLORD, *
     which they hurled at the ˈheels of ˈyour aˈnointed.

Edward John Hopkins
Descant: Sydney Nicholson

205

Use in setting 2.

†52 Blessèd be the LORD for ˈever ˈmore! *
     A ˈmen, I ˈsay, A ˈmen.

When required, Gloria Patri may be sung to #201 in setting 1; to #202 in setting 2.

Psalm 90   *Domine, refugium*

206

Ray Francis Brown

207

"St. Anne" *John Bertalot*

1 Lord, you have'been our'refuge *
   from one gene'ration'to a'nother.

2 Before the mountains were brought forth,
   or the land and the'earth were'born, *
   from age to'age'you are'God.

3 You turn us back to the'dust and'say, *
   "Go'back, O'child of'earth."

4 For a thousand years in your sight are like yesterday'when it is'past *
   and'like a'watch in the'night.

5 You sweep us a'way like a'dream; *
   we fade away'suddenly'like the'grass.

6 In the morning it is'green and'flourishes; *
   in the evening it is'dried'up and'withered.

7 For we consume away in'your dis'pleasure; *
   we are afraid because of your'wrathful'indig'nation.

8 Our iniquities you have'set be'fore you, *
   and our secret'sins in the'light of your'countenance.

9 When you are angry, all our'days are'gone: *
    we bring our years to an'end'like a'sigh.

10 The span of our life is seventy years,
    perhaps in strength'even'eighty; *
      yet the sum of them is but labor and sorrow,
      for they pass away'quickly and'we are'gone.

11 Who regards the'power of your'wrath? *
    who rightly'fears your'indig'nation?

12 So teach us to'number our'days *
    that we may ap'ply our'hearts to'wisdom.

13 Return, O LORD; how'long will you'tarry? *
    be'gracious'to your'servants.

14 Satisfy us by your loving'kindness in the'morning; *
    so shall we rejoice and be'glad all the'days of our'life.

15 Make us glad by the measure of the'days that you af'flicted us *
    and the years in'which we'suffered ad'versity.

16 Show your'servants your'works *
    and your'splendor'to their'children.

†17 May the graciousness of the LORD our'God be up'on us; *
    prosper the work of our'hands;'
    'prosper our'handiwork.

Psalm 91   *Qui habitat*

208   *John Goss*

209   *Edward John Hopkins*

1 He who dwells in the shelter of the ˈMöst ˈHigh, *
   abides under the ˈshadow ˈof the Alˈmighty.

2 He shall say to the LORD,
   "You are my ˈrefuge and my ˈstronghold, *
   my God in ˈwhom I ˈput my ˈtrust."

3 He shall deliver you from the ˈsnare of the ˈhunter *
   and ˈfrom the ˈdeadly ˈpestilence.

4 He shall cover you with his pinions,
   and you shall find refuge ˈunder his ˈwings; *
   his faithfulness shall ˈbe a ˈshield and ˈbuckler.

5 You shall not be afraid of any ˈterror by ˈnight, *
   nor of the ˈarrow that ˈflies by ˈday;

6 Of the plague that ˈstalks in the ˈdarkness, *
   nor of the sickness that ˈläys ˈwaste at ˈmid-day.

7 A thousand shall fall at your side
   and ten thousand at ˈyour right ˈhand, *
   but ˈit shall ˈnot come ˈnear you.

8 Your eyes have ˈonly to be ˈhold *
   to ˈsee the reˈward of the ˈwicked.

9 Because you have made the |LORD your |refuge, *

 and the Most |High your |habi|tation,

10 There shall no evil |happen to |you, *

 neither shall any |plague come |near your |dwelling.

11 For he shall give his angels |charge |over you, *

 to |keep you in |all your |ways.

12 They shall |bear you in their |hands, *

 lest you dash your |foot a|gainst a |stone.

13 You shall tread upon the |lion and |adder; *

 you shall trample the young lion and the |serpent |under your |feet.

14 Because he is bound to me in love,

 therefore will |I de|liver him; *

 I will protect him, be|cause he |knows my |Name.

15 He shall call upon me, and |I will |answer him; *

 I am with him in trouble;

 I will |rescue him and |bring him to |honor.

16 With long |life will I |satisfy him, *

 and |show him |my sal|vation.

Psalm 92 *Bonum est confiteri*

210   *John Goss*

211   *John Barnard*

1 It is a good thing to give 'thanks to the 'LORD, *
      and to sing praises to your 'Näme, 'O Most 'High;

2 To tell of your loving-kindness 'early in the 'morning *
      and of your 'faithfulness 'in the night 'season;

3 On the psaltery, and 'on the 'lyre, *
      and to the 'melody 'of the 'harp.

4 For you have made me glad by your 'acts, O 'LORD; *
      and I shout for joy because of the 'wörks 'of your 'hands.

5 LORD, how 'great are your 'works! *
      your 'thoughts are 'very 'deep.

6 The dullard does not know,
      nor does the 'fool under'stand, *
         that though the wicked grow like weeds,
         and all the 'workers of in'iquity 'flourish,

7 They flourish only to be de'stroyed for 'ever; *
      but you, O LORD, are ex'alted for 'ever'more.

8 For lo, your enemies, O LORD,
      lo, your 'enemies shall 'perish, *
         and all the workers of in'iquity 'shall be 'scattered.

9 But my horn you have exalted like the horns of |wĭld |bulls; *
   I am a |nointed with |frĕsh |oil.

10 My eyes also gloat |over my |enemies, *
   and my ears rejoice to hear the doom of
                     the |wicked who |rise up a |gainst me.

11 The righteous shall |flourish like a |palm tree, *
   and shall spread a |broad like a |cedar of |Lebanon.

12 Those who are planted in the |house of the |LORD *
   shall |flourish in the |courts of our |God;

13 They shall still bear fruit in |ŏld |age; *
   they |shall be |green and |succulent;

14 That they may show how |upright the |LORD is, *
   my Rock, in |whom there |is no |fault.

Psalm 93 *Dominus regnavit*

212

Sydney Nicholson

213

George Elvey

1 The LORD is King;
he has put on 'splendid ap'parel; *
    the LORD has put on his apparel
    and 'girded him'self with 'strength.

2 He has made the whole 'world so 'sure *
    — 'that it 'cannot be 'moved;

3 Ever since the world began, your throne has 'been es'tablished; *
    you 'are from 'ever'lasting.

4 The waters have lifted up, O LORD,
    the waters have lifted 'up their 'voice; *
    the waters have lifted 'up their 'pounding 'waves.

5 Mightier than the sound of many waters,
    mightier than the 'breakers of the 'sea, *
    mightier is the 'LORD who 'dwells on 'high.

6 Your testimonies are 'very 'sure, *
    and holiness adorns your house, O LORD,
    for ever 'and for 'ever'more.

Psalm 94   *Deus ultionum*

214   *Joseph Barnby*

215   *Charles Villiers Stanford*

1   O LORD|God of|vengeance, *
      O God of|vengeance,|show your|self.

2   Rise up, O|Judge of the|world; *
      give the|arrogant their|just de|serts.

3   How long shall the|wicked, O|LORD, *
      how|long shall the|wicked|triumph?

4   They|bluster in their|insolence; *
      all evil|doers are|full of|boasting.

5   They crush your|people, O|LORD, *
      and af|flict your|chosen|nation.

6   They murder the|widow and the|stranger *
      and|put the|orphans to|death.

7   Yet they say, "The|LORD does not|see, *
      the God of|Jacob|takes no|notice."

8   Consider well, you dullards a|mong the|people; *
      when|will you|fools under|stand?

214   *Joseph Barnby*

215   *Charles Villiers Stanford*

9 He that planted the ear, 'does he not 'hear? *
    he that formed the 'eÿe 'does he not 'see?

10 He who admonishes the nations, will 'he not 'punish? *
    he who teaches all the 'world, has 'he no 'knowledge?

†11 The LORD knows our 'human 'thoughts; *
    how like a 'puff of 'wind they 'are.

12 Happy are they whom you in'struct, O 'Lord! *
    whom you 'teäch 'out of your 'law;

13 To give them rest in 'evil 'days, *
    until a 'pit is 'dug for the 'wicked.

14 For the LORD will not a'bandon his 'people, *
    nor 'will he for'sake his 'own.

15 For judgment will a'gain be 'just, *
    and all the 'true of 'heart will 'follow it.

16 Who rose up for me a'gainst the 'wicked? *
    who took my part a'gainst the 'evil'doers?

17 If the LORD had not 'come to my 'help, *
    I should soon have 'dwelt in the 'land of 'silence.

18 As often as I said, "My|foot has|slipped," *
  your|love, O|LORD, up|held me.

19 When many cares|fill my|mind, *
  your conso|lations|cheer my|soul.

20 Can a corrupt tribunal have any|part with|you, *
  one which frames|evil|into|law?

21 They conspire against the|life of the|just *
  and con|demn the|innocent to|death.

22 But the LORD has be|come my|stronghold, *
  and my|God the|rock of my|trust.

23 He will turn their wickedness back upon them
  and destroy them in their|own|malice; *
  the|LORD our|God will de|stroy them.

Psalm 95   *Venite, exultemus*

216

Robert Prescott Stewart

217

Richard Wayne Dirksen

1 Come, let us ⌐sing to the⌐ LORD; *
   let us shout for joy to the⌐ Rock of⌐ our sal⌐ vation.

2 Let us come before his⌐ presence with thanks⌐ giving *
   and raise a loud⌐ shout to⌐ him with⌐ psalms.

3 For the LORD is a⌐ grëat⌐ God, *
   and a great⌐ King a⌐ bove all⌐ gods.

4 In his hand are the⌐ caverns of the⌐ earth, *
   and the heights of the⌐ hills are⌐ hïs⌐ also.

†5 The sea is⌐ his, for he⌐ made it, *
   and his hands have⌐ molded the⌐ dry⌐ land.

6 Come, let us bow down, and'bend the'knee, *
   and'kneel before the'LORD our'Maker.

7 For he is our God,
   and we are the people of his pasture and the'sheep of his'hand. *
    Oh, that to'day you would'hearken to his'voice!

8 Harden not your hearts,
   as your forebears'did in the'wilderness, *
    at Meribah, and on that day at'Massah,'
    'when they'tempted me.

9 They'put me to the'test, *
   —'though they had'seen my'works.

10 Forty years long I detested that gene'ration and'said, *
   "This people are wayward in their hearts;
   'they do not'know my'ways."

11 So I'swore in my'wrath, *
   "They shall not'enter'into my'rest."

Psalm 96 *Cantate Domino*

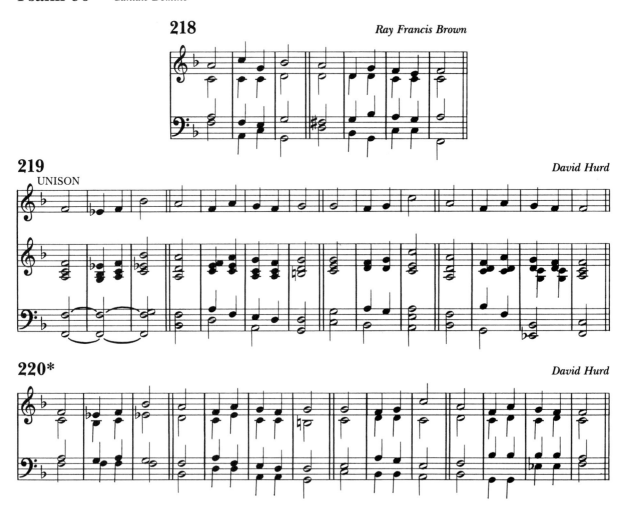

218   *Ray Francis Brown*

219   *David Hurd*

UNISON

220*   *David Hurd*

1 Sing to the LORD a|nĕw|song; *
   sing to the LORD,|all the|whŏle|earth.

2 Sing to the LORD and|bless his|Name; *
   proclaim the good news of his sal|vation from|day to|day.

3 Declare his glory a|mong the|nations *
   and his|wonders a|mong all|peoples.

4 For great is the LORD and|greatly to be|praised; *
   he is more to be|feared than|äll|gods.

†5 As for all the gods of the nations,|they are but|idols; *
   but it is the|LORD who|made the|heavens.

*Note: If #220 is to be sung, the organ should play the accompaniment given at #219.

6 Oh, the majesty and mag|nificence of his|presence! *
   Oh, the power and the|splendor|of his|sanctuary!

7 Ascribe to the LORD, you|families of the|peoples; *
   ascribe to the|LÖRD|honor and|power.

8 Ascribe to the LORD the honor|due his|Name; *
   bring offerings and|come in|to his|courts.

9 Worship the LORD in the|beauty of|holiness; *
   let the|whole earth|tremble be|fore him.

10 Tell it out among the nations: "The|LORD is|King! *
   he has made the world so firm that it cannot be moved;
   he will|judge the|peoples with|equity."

11 Let the heavens rejoice, and let the earth be glad;
   let the sea thunder and|all that is|in it; *
   let the field be joyful and|all that|is there|in.

12 Then shall all the trees of the wood shout for joy
   before the|LORD when he|comes, *
   when he|comes to|judge the|earth.

13 He will judge the|world with|righteousness *
   and the|peoples|with his|truth.

Psalm 97 *Dominus regnavit*

221 *Henry Thomas Smart*

222 *Walter Parratt*

1 The LORD is King;
  let the|earth re|joice; *
    let the|multitude of the|isles be|glad.

2 Clouds and darkness are|round a|bout him, *
    righteousness and justice are the foun|dations|of his|throne.

3 A fire|goes be|fore him *
    and burns up his|enemies on|every|side.

4 His lightnings light|up the|world; *
    the earth|sees it and|is a|fraid.

5 The mountains melt like wax at the|presence of the|LORD, *
    at the presence of the|Lord of the|whöle|earth.

6 The heavens de|clare his|righteousness, *
    and all the|peoples|see his|glory.

7 Confounded be all who worship carved images
  and delight in|false|gods! *
    Bow down be|fore him,|all you|gods.

8 Zion hears and is glad, and the cities of|Judah re|joice, *
    be|cause of your|judgments, O|LORD.

212

9 For you are the LORD,
  most high over'all the'earth; *
    you are exalted'far above'äll'gods.

10 The LORD loves'those who hate'evil; *
  he preserves the lives of his saints
    and delivers them from the'händ'of the'wicked.

11 Light has sprung'up for the'righteous, *
  and joyful gladness for'those who are'trüe'hearted.

12 Rejoice in the'LORD, you'righteous, *
  and give'thanks to his'holy'Name.

Psalm 98   *Cantate Domino*

223   *George A. Macfarren*

224   *Ivor Algernon Atkins*

1 Sing to the LORD a'nëw'song, *
  for'he has done'marvelous'things.

2 With his right hand and his'holy'arm *
  has he'won for him'self the'victory.

3 The LORD has made'known his'victory; *
  his righteousness has he openly'shown in the'sight of the'nations.

4 He remembers his mercy and faithfulness to the'house of'Israel, *
  and all the ends of the earth have seen the'victory'of our'God.

223

George A. Macfarren

224

Ivor Algernon Atkins

5 Shout with joy to the LORD ' all you ' lands; *
   lift up your ' voice, re ' joice, and ' sing.

6 Sing to the ' LORD with the ' harp, *
   with the ' harp and the ' voice of ' song.

7 With trumpets and the ' sound of the ' horn *
   shout with joy be ' fore the ' King, the ' LORD.

8 Let the sea make a noise and ' all that is ' in it, *
   the lands and ' those who ' dwell there ' in.

9 Let the rivers ' clap their ' hands, *
   and let the hills ring out with joy before the LORD,
   when he ' comes to ' judge the ' earth.

10 In righteousness shall he ' judge the ' world *
   — ' and the ' peoples with ' equity.

Psalm 99   *Dominus regnavit*

225   *Thomas Tallis*

226   *Thomas Attwood*

1 The LORD is King;
    let the ⁣'people ⁣'tremble; *
        he is enthroned upon the cherubim;
        'let the 'eärth 'shake.

2 The LORD is 'great in 'Zion; *
        he is 'high a'bove all 'peoples.

†3 Let them confess his Name, which is 'great and 'awesome; *
        —'he is the 'Holy 'One.

4 "O mighty King, lover of justice,
    you have es'tablished 'equity; *
        you have executed justice and 'righteous'ness in 'Jacob."

5 Proclaim the greatness of the LORD our God
    and fall 'down before his 'footstool; *
        —'he is the 'Holy 'One.

6 Moses and Aaron among his priests,
    and Samuel among those who 'call upon his 'Name, *
        they called upon the 'LÖRD, 'and he 'answered them.

215

225

Thomas Tallis

226

Thomas Attwood

7 He spoke to them out of the 'pillar of 'cloud; *
   they kept his testimonies and the de'crëe 'that he 'gave them.

8 "O LORD our God, you 'answered them in 'deed; *
   you were a God who forgave them,
   yet punished them 'for their 'evil 'deeds."

9 Proclaim the greatness of the LORD our God
   and worship him upon his 'holy 'hill; *
   for the 'LORD our 'God is the 'Holy One.

Psalm 100 *Jubilate Deo*

227 *John Stainer*

228 *Francis Jackson*

1 Be joyful in the LORD, 'all you 'lands; *
   serve the LORD with gladness
   and come before his 'presence 'with a 'song.

2 Know this: The LORD him 'self is 'God; *
   he himself has made us, and we are his;
   we are his 'people and the 'sheep of his 'pasture.

3 Enter his gates with thanksgiving;
   go into his 'courts with 'praise; *
   give thanks to him and 'call up'on his 'Name.

4 For the LORD is good;
   his mercy is 'ever'lasting; *
   and his faithfulness en'dures from 'age to 'age.

Psalm 101   *Misericordiam et judicium*

229
Thomas Jackson

230 David Hurd

1 I will sing of⌐mercy and⌐justice; *
to you, O⌐LORD, will⌐I sing⌐praises.

2 I will strive to follow a blameless course;
oh,⌐when will you⌐come to me? *
I will walk with sincerity of⌐heart with⌐in my⌐house.

3 I will set no worthless thing be⌐fore my⌐eyes; *
I hate the doers of evil deeds;
⌐they shall⌐not re⌐main with me.

4 A crooked⌐heart shall be⌐far from me; *
I⌐will not⌐knöw⌐evil.

5 Those who in secret slander their neighbors I⌐will de⌐stroy; *
those who have a haughty look and a proud⌐heart I⌐cannot a⌐bide.

6 My eyes are upon the faithful in the land, that⌐they may⌐dwell with me, *
and only those who lead a blameless⌐life shall⌐be my⌐servants.

7 Those who act deceitfully shall not⌐dwell in my⌐house, *
and those who tell lies shall not con⌐tinue⌐in my⌐sight.

8 I will soon destroy all the⌐wicked in the⌐land, *
that I may root out all evildoers from the⌐city⌐of the⌐LORD.

Psalm 102   *Domine, exaudi*

231

William Crotch

232

David Hurd

1 LORD, hear my prayer, and let my cry ' come be ' fore you; *
  hide not your face from ' me in the ' day of my ' trouble.

2 In ' cline your ' ear to me; *
  when I ' call, make ' haste to ' answer me,

3 For my days drift a ' way like ' smoke, *
  and my bones are ' hot as ' burning ' coals.

4 My heart is smitten like ' grass and ' withered, *
  so that I for ' get to ' eat my ' bread.

5 Because of the ' voice of my ' groaning *
  — ' I am but ' skin and ' bones.

6 I have become like a ' vulture in the ' wilderness, *
  like an ' owl a ' mong the ' ruins.

7 I lie a ' wake and ' groan; *
  I am like a sparrow, ' lonely ' on a ' house-top.

8 My enemies revile me ' all day ' long, *
  and those who scoff at me have ' taken an ' oath a ' gainst me.

231   *William Crotch*

232   *David Hurd*

9 For I have eaten⎰ashes for⎰bread *
    and⎰mingled my⎰drink with⎰weeping.

10 Because of your indig⎰nation and⎰wrath *
    you have lifted me⎰up and⎰thrown me a⎰way.

11 My days pass a⎰way like a⎰shadow, *
    and I⎰wither⎰like the⎰grass.

12 But you, O LORD, en⎰dure for⎰ever, *
    and your⎰Name from⎰age to⎰age.

13 You will arise and have compassion on Zion,
    for it is time to have⎰mercy up⎰on her; *
    indeed, the ap⎰pointed⎰time has⎰come.

14 For your servants love her⎰very⎰rubble, *
    and are moved to pity⎰even⎰for her⎰dust.

15 The nations shall fear your⎰Name, O⎰LORD, *
    and all the⎰kings of the⎰earth your⎰glory.

16 For the LORD will⎰build up⎰Zion, *
    and his⎰glory⎰will ap⎰pear.

17 He will look with favor on the'prayer of the'homeless; *
    he'will not de'spise their'plea.

18 Let this be written for a future'gene'ration, *
    so that a people yet un'born may'praise the'LORD.

19 For the LORD looked down from his holy'place on'high; *
    from the'heavens he be'held the'earth;

20 That he might hear the'groan of the'captive *
    and set free'those con'demned to'die;

21 That they may declare in Zion the'Name of the'LORD, *
    and his'präise'in Je'rusalem;

22 When the peoples are'gathered to'gether, *
    and the kingdoms'also, to'serve the'LORD.

23 He has brought down my strength be'fore my'time; *
    he has shortened the'number'of my'days;

24 And I said, "O my God,
    do not take me away in the'midst of my'days; *
    your years endure throughout'äll'gene'rations.

25 In the beginning, O LORD, you laid the foun'dations of the'earth, *
    and the'heavens are the'work of your'hands;

26 They shall perish, but you will endure;
    they all shall wear'out like a'garment; *
    as clothing you will'change them,
    and'they shall be'changed;

27 But you are'always the'same, *
    and your'years will'never'end.

28 The children of your'servants shall con'tinue, *
    and their offspring shall'städn'fast in your'sight."

Psalm 103   *Benedic, anima mea*

233   *Kellow J. Pye*

234   *John Camidge II*

1 Bless the LORD, ' O my ' soul, *
   and all that is within me, ' bless his ' holy ' Name.

2 Bless the LORD, ' O my ' soul, *
   and for ' get not ' all his ' benefits.

3 He forgives ' all your ' sins *
   and ' heäls ' all your in ' firmities;

4 He redeems your ' life from the ' grave *
   and crowns you with ' mercy and ' loving ' kindness;

†5 He satisfies you with ' göod ' things, *
   and your ' youth is re ' newed like an ' eagle's.

6 The LORD ' executes ' righteousness *
   and judgment for ' all who ' are op ' pressed.

7 He made his ways ' known to ' Moses *
   and his ' works to the ' children of ' Israel.

8 The LORD is full of com ' passion and ' mercy, *
   slow to ' anger and of ' grëat ' kindness.

9 He will not ' always ac ' cuse us, *
   nor will he ' keep his ' anger for ' ever.

†10 He has not dealt with us ac'cording to our'sins, *
  nor rewarded us ac'cording'to our'wickedness.

11 For as the heavens are'high above the'earth, *
  so is his mercy'great upon'those who'fear him.

12 As far as the'east is from the'west, *
  so far has he re'moved our'sins'from us.

13 As a father'cares for his'children, *
  so does the LORD'care for'those who'fear him.

14 For he himself knows where'of we are'made; *
  he re'members that'we are but'dust.

15 Our days are'like the'grass; *
  we flourish like a'flower'of the'field;

16 When the wind goes over it,'it is'gone, *
  and its'place shall'know it no'more.

17 But the merciful goodness of the LORD endures for
      ever on'those who'fear him, *
  and his'righteousness on'children's'children;

18 On those who'keep his'covenant *
  and remember'his com'mandments and'do them.

19 The LORD has set his'throne in'heaven, *
  and his kingship has do'minion'over'all.

20 Bless the LORD, you angels of his,
  you mighty ones who'do his'bidding, *
  and'hearken to the'voice of his'word.

21 Bless the LORD, all'you his'hosts, *
  you ministers of'his who'do his'will.

22 Bless the LORD, all you works of his,
  in all places of'his do'minion; *
  bless the'LÖRD,'O my'soul.

Psalm 104   *Benedic, anima mea*

235

William Crotch

236

Edward Cuthbert Bairstow

Setting 1: #235; setting 2: #236–237.

1 Bless the LORD, 'O my 'soul; *
   O LORD my God, how excellent is your greatness!
   you are 'clothed with 'majesty and 'splendor.

2 You wrap yourself with 'light as with a 'cloak *
   and spread out the 'heavens 'like a 'curtain.

3 You lay the beams of your chambers in the 'waters a'bove; *
   you make the clouds your chariot;
   you 'ride on the 'wings of the 'wind.

4 You make the 'winds your 'messengers *
   and 'flames of 'fire your 'servants.

5 You have set the earth up'on its foun'dations, *
   so that it never shall 'move at 'any 'time.

6 You covered it with the 'Deep as with a 'mantle; *
   the waters stood 'higher 'than the 'mountains.

7 At your re'buke they 'fled; *
   at the voice of your 'thunder they 'hastened a'way.

8 They went up into the hills and down to the 'valleys be'neath, *
   to the places 'you had ap'pointed 'for them.

9 You set the limits that they'should not'pass; *
   they shall'not again'cover the'earth.

10 You send the'springs into the'valleys; *
   they'flow be'tween the'mountains.

11 All the beasts of the field'drink their'fill from them, *
   and the wild'asses'quench their'thirst.

12 Beside them the birds of the air'make their'nests *
   and'sing a'mong the'branches.

13 You water the mountains from your'dwelling on'high; *
   the earth is fully satisfied by the'fruit'of your'works.

14 You make grass grow for'flocks and'herds *
   and'plants to'serve man'kind;

15 That they may bring forth'food from the'earth, *
   and'wine to'gladden our'hearts,

16 Oil to make a'cheerful'countenance, *
   and'bread to'strengthen the'heart.

17 The trees of the LORD are'full of'sap, *
   the cedars of'Lebanon'which he'planted,

18 In which the'birds build their'nests, *
   and in whose tops the'stork'makes his'dwelling.

19 The high hills are a refuge for the'mountain'goats, *
   and the'stony'cliffs for the'rock badgers.

20 You appointed the moon to'mark the'seasons, *
   and the sun'knows the'time of its'setting.

21 You make darkness that it'may be'night, *
   in which all the'beasts of the'forest'prowl.

22 The lions roar'after their'prey *
   and'seek their'food from'God.

23 The sun rises, and they'slip a'way *
   and'lay themselves'down in their'dens.

24 Man goes'forth to his'work *
   and to his'labor un'til the'evening.

235

William Crotch

237

Edward Cuthbert Bairstow

25 O LORD, how ˈmanifold are yourˈworks! *
    in wisdom you have made them all;
    theˈearth isˈfull of yourˈcreatures.

26 Yonder is the great and wide sea
    with its living things tooˈmany toˈnumber, *
    —ˈcreatures bothˈsmall andˈgreat.

27 There move the ships,
    and there isˈthat Leˈviathan, *
    whichˈyou haveˈmade for theˈsport of it.

28 All of themˈlook toˈyou *
    to give them theirˈfood inˈdüeˈseason.

29 You give it toˈthem; theyˈgather it; *
    you open your hand, andˈthey areˈfilled withˈgood things.

30 You hide your face, andˈthey areˈterrified; *
    you take away their breath,
    and theyˈdie and reˈturn to theirˈdust.

†31 You send forth your Spirit, andˈthey are creˈated; *
    and so you reˈnew theˈface of theˈearth.

32 May the glory of the LORD en'dure for'ever; *
    may the LORD re'joice in'all his'works.

33 He looks at the'earth and it'trembles; *
    he touches the'mountains'and they'smoke.

34 I will sing to the LORD as'long as I'live; *
    I will praise my'God while I'have my'being.

35 May these words of'mine'please him; *
    I will re'joice'in the'LORD.

36 Let sinners be consumed'out of the'earth, *
    and the'wicked'be no'more.

37 Bless the LORD,'O my'soul. *
    —'Halle'lü'jah!

Psalm 105: Part 1 *Confitemini Domino*

238

Stephen Elvey

240

David Hurd

Setting 1: #238–239; setting 2: #240–241.

1 Give thanks to the LORD and ꞏcall upon his ꞏName; *
  make known his ꞏdeeds a ꞏmong the ꞏpeoples.

2 Sing to him, sing ꞏpraises to ꞏhim, *
  and speak of ꞏall his ꞏmarvelous ꞏworks.

3 Glory in his ꞏholy ꞏName; *
  let the hearts of those who ꞏseek the ꞏLORD re ꞏjoice.

4 Search for the ꞏLORD and his ꞏstrength; *
  con ꞏtinually ꞏseek his ꞏface.

5 Remember the ꞏmarvels he has ꞏdone, *
  his wonders and the ꞏjudgments ꞏof his ꞏmouth,

6 O offspring of ꞏAbraham his ꞏservant, *
  O ꞏchildren of ꞏJacob his ꞏchosen.

7 He is the ꞏLORD our ꞏGod; *
  his judgments pre ꞏvail in ꞏall the ꞏworld.

8 He has always been ꞏmindful of his ꞏcovenant, *
  the promise he made for a ꞏthousand ꞏgene ꞏrations:

9 The covenant he'made with'Abraham, *
  the'oath that he'swore to'Isaac,

10 Which he established as a'statute for'Jacob, *
  an everlasting'cove'nant for'Israel,

11 Saying, "To you will I give the'land of'Canaan *
  to'be your al'lotted in'heritance."

12 When they were'few in'number, *
  of little account, and'sojourners'in the'land,

13 Wandering from'nation to'nation *
  and from one'kingdom'to an'other,

14 He let'no one op'press them *
  and re'büked'kings for their'sake,

†15 Saying, "Do not'touch my a'nointed *
  and'do my'prophets no'harm."

16 Then he called for a'famine in the'land *
  and de'stroyed the sup'ply of'bread.

17 He sent a'man be'fore them, *
  —'Joseph, who was'sold as a'slave.

18 They bruised his'feet in'fetters; *
  his neck they'put in an'iron'collar.

19 Until his prediction'came to'pass, *
  the'word of the'LÖRD'tested him.

20 The king'sent and re'leased him; *
  the ruler of the'peoples'set him'free.

21 He set him as a master'over his'household, *
  as a'ruler over'all his pos'sessions,

†22 To instruct his princes ac'cording to his'will *
  and to'teach his'elders'wisdom.

Psalm 105: Part 2 *Et intravit Israel*

239 *Alec Wyton*

241 *David Hurd*

23 Israel⌐came into⌐Egypt, *
  and Jacob became a⌐sojourner in the⌐land of⌐Ham.

24 The LORD made his people ex⌐ceedingly⌐fruitful; *
  he made them⌐stronger⌐than their⌐enemies;

25 Whose heart he turned, so that they⌐hated his⌐people, *
  and dealt un⌐justly⌐with his⌐servants.

26 He sent⌐Moses his⌐servant, *
  and⌐Aaron whom⌐he had⌐chosen.

27 They worked his⌐signs a⌐mong them, *
  and⌐portents in the⌐land of⌐Ham.

28 He sent darkness, and⌐it grew⌐dark; *
  but the Egyptians re⌐belled a⌐gainst his⌐words.

29 He turned their⌐waters into⌐blood *
  and⌐caused their⌐fish to⌐die.

30 Their land was over⌐run by⌐frogs, *
  in the very⌐chambers⌐of their⌐kings.

31 He spoke, and there came'swarms of'insects *
   and'gnats within'all their'borders.

32 He gave them hailstones in'stead of'rain, *
   and flames of'fire through'out their'land.

33 He blasted their'vines and their'fig trees *
   and'shattered every'tree in their'country.

34 He spoke, and the'locust'came, *
   and young'locusts with'oüt'number,

35 Which ate up all the green'plants in their'land *
   and de'voured the'fruit of their'soil.

36 He struck down the'firstborn of their'land, *
   the'firstfruits of'all their'strength.

238

Stephen Elvey

240

David Hurd

238

Stephen Elvey

240

David Hurd

37 He led out his people with ˈsilver and ˈgold; *
    in all their tribes there was ˈnöt ˈone that ˈstumbled.

38 Egypt was ˈglad of their ˈgoing, *
    beˈcause they ˈwere aˈfraid of them.

39 He spread out a ˈcloud for a ˈcovering *
    and a fire to give ˈlight in the ˈnight ˈseason.

40 They asked, and ˈquails apˈpeared, *
    and he satisfied ˈthem with ˈbread from ˈheaven.

41 He opened the rock, and ˈwater ˈflowed, *
    so the river ˈran in the ˈdry ˈplaces.

42 For God remembered his ˈholy ˈword *
    and ˈAbraˈham his ˈservant.

†43 So he led forth his ˈpeople with ˈgladness, *
    his ˈchosen with ˈshouts of ˈjoy.

44 He gave his people the ˈlands of the ˈnations, *
    and they took the ˈfruit of ˈothers' ˈtoil.

45 That they might ˈkeep his ˈstatutes *
    and observe his ˈläws. ˈ Halleˈlujah!

Psalm 106: Part 1 *Confitemini Domino*

242 *Thomas Jackson*

244 *Alec Wyton*

Setting 1: #242–243; setting 2: #244–245.

1 Hallelujah!
   Give thanks to the LORD, for ˈhe is ˈgood, *
      for his ˈmercy enˈdures for ˈever.

2 Who can declare the mighty ˈacts of the ˈLORD *
      or ˈshow forth ˈall his ˈpraise?

3 Happy are those who ˈact with ˈjustice *
      and ˈalways ˈdo what is ˈright!

4 Remember me, O LORD, with the favor you ˈhave for your ˈpeople, *
      and visit me ˈwith your ˈsaving ˈhelp;

†5 That I may see the prosperity of your elect
   and be glad with the ˈgladness of your ˈpeople, *
      that I may ˈglory with ˈyour inˈheritance.

6 We have sinned as our ˈforebears ˈdid; *
      we have done ˈwrong and ˈdëalt ˈwickedly.

7 In Egypt they did not consider your marvelous works,
   nor remember the aˈbundance of your ˈlove; *
      they defied the Most ˈHigh at the ˈRëd ˈSea.

242

T. Jackson

244

Alec Wyton

8 But he saved them for his'Näme's'sake, *
    to'make his'power'known.

9 He rebuked the Red Sea, and it'drïed'up, *
    and he led them through the'deep as'through a'desert.

10 He saved them from the hand of'those who'hated them *
    and re'deemed them from the'hand of the'enemy.

11 The waters'covered their op'pressors; *
    not'one of'them was'left.

†12 Then they be'lieved his'words *
    and'sang him'songs of'praise.

243

Alec Wyton

245

Andrew Seivewright

13 But they soon for⎸got his⎸deeds *
  and⎸did not⎸wait for his⎸counsel.

14 A craving⎸seized them in the⎸wilderness, *
  and they put⎸God to the⎸test in the⎸desert.

15 He⎸gave them what they⎸asked, *
  but sent⎸leanness⎸into their⎸soul.

16 They envied⎸Moses in the⎸camp, *
  and Aaron, the⎸holy⎸one of the⎸LORD.

17 The earth opened and⎸swallowed⎸Dathan *
  and⎸covered the⎸company of Ab⎸iram.

18 Fire blazed up a⎸gainst their⎸company, *
  and⎸flames de⎸voured the⎸wicked.

Psalm 106: Part 2   *Et fecerunt vitulum*

243

Alec Wyton

245

Andrew Seivewright

19 Israel made a⌐bull-calf at⌐Horeb *
   and⌐worshiped a⌐molten⌐image;

20 And so they ex⌐changed their⌐Glory *
   for the image of an⌐ox that⌐feeds on⌐grass.

21 They forgot⌐God their⌐Savior, *
   who had done⌐grëat⌐things in⌐Egypt,

22 Wonderful deeds in the⌐land of⌐Ham, *
   and fearful⌐things at the⌐Rëd⌐Sea.

23 So he would have destroyed them,
   had not Moses his chosen stood be⌐fore him in the⌐breach, *
   to turn a⌐way his⌐wrath from con⌐suming them.

24 They refused the⌐pleasant⌐land *
   and⌐would not be⌐lieve his⌐promise.

†25 They⌐grumbled in their⌐tents *
   and would not⌐listen to the⌐voice of the⌐LORD.

26 So he lifted his⌐hand a⌐gainst them, *
   to over⌐throw them⌐in the⌐wilderness,

27 To cast out their⌐seed among the⌐nations, *
   and to⌐scatter them through⌐out the⌐lands.

236

28 They joined themselves to ' Bäal ! Peor *
   and ate sacrifices ' offered ' to the ' dead.

29 They provoked him to ' anger with their ' actions, *
   and a ' plague broke ' out a ' mong them.

30 Then Phinehas stood up and ' inter ' ceded, *
   and the ' plägue ' came to an ' end.

31 This was reckoned to ' him as ' righteousness *
   throughout ' all gene ' rations for ' ever.

32 Again they provoked his anger at the ' waters of ' Meribah, *
   so that he ' punished ' Moses be ' cause of them;

33 For they so em ' bittered his ' spirit *
   that he spoke ' räsh ' words with his ' lips.

34 They did not de ' stroy the ' peoples *
   — ' as the ' LORD had com ' manded them.

35 They inter ' mingled with the ' heathen *
   and ' learned their ' pagan ' ways,

36 So that they ' worshiped their ' idols, *
   — ' which be ' came a ' snare to them.

37 They ' sacrificed their ' sons *
   and their ' daughters to ' evil ' spirits.

38 They shed innocent blood,
   the blood of their ' sons and ' daughters, *
      which they offered to the idols of Canaan,
      and the ' land was de ' filed with ' blood.

39 Thus they were pol ' luted by their ' actions *
   and went ' whoring in their ' evil ' deeds.

40 Therefore the wrath of the LORD was kindled a ' gainst his ' people *
   and ' he ab ' horred his in ' heritance.

41 He gave them over to the ' hand of the ' heathen, *
   and those who ' hated ' them ruled ' over them.

243

Alec Wyton

245

Andrew Seivewright

42 Their ' enemies op ' pressed them, *
    and they were ' humbled ' under their ' hand.

43 Many a time did he deliver them,
    but they rebelled through their ' own de ' vices, *
    and were brought ' down in ' their in ' iquity.

44 Nevertheless, he ' saw their dis ' tress, *
    when he ' heard their ' lamen ' tation.

45 He remembered his ' covenant with ' them *
    and relented in ac ' cordance with ' his great ' mercy.

†46 He ' caused them to be ' pitied *
    by ' those who ' held them ' captive.

242

Thomas Jackson

244

Alec Wyton

47 Save us, O LORD our God,
   and gather us from a'mong the'nations, *
      that we may give thanks to your holy Name
      and'glory'in your'praise.

48 Blessèd be the LORD, the God of Israel,
   from everlasting and to'ever'lasting; *
      and let all the people say, "A'mën!"'
      'Halle'lujah!

Psalm 107: Part 1   *Confitemini Domino*

246   *Jonathan Battishill*   **249**   *Ray Francis Brown*

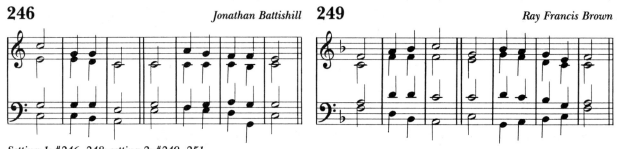

Setting 1: #246–248; setting 2: #249–251.

1 Give thanks to the LORD, for'he is'good, *
    and his'mercy en'dures for'ever.

2 Let all those whom the LORD has re'deemed pro'claim *
    that he re'deemed them from the'hand of the'foe.

3 He gathered them'out of the'lands; *
    from the east and from the west,
    from the'north and'from the'south.

247   *William Savage*   **250**   *John Blow*

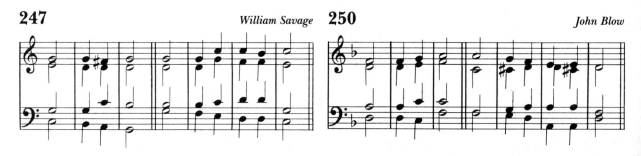

4 Some wandered in'desert'wastes; *
    they found no way to a'city where'they might'dwell.

5 They were'hungry and'thirsty; *
    their'spirits'languished with'in them.

6 Then they cried to the'LORD in their'trouble, *
    and he de'livered them from'their dis'tress.

7 He put their feet on a'sträight'path *
    to go to a'city where'they might'dwell.

248   *William Crotch*

251   *Thomas Attwood*

8 Let them give thanks to the ⌐LORD for his⌐ mercy *
   and the ⌐wonders he⌐ does for his ⌐children.

9 For he ⌐satisfies the ⌐thirsty *
   and ⌐fills the ⌐hungry with ⌐good things.

247   *William Savage*   **250**   *John Blow*

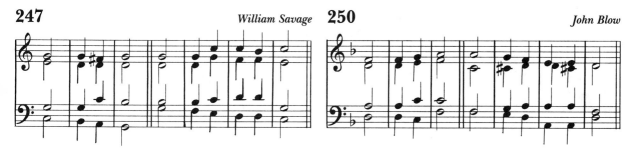

10 Some sat in darkness and⌐dëep⌐gloom, *
    bound⌐fast in⌐misery and⌐iron;

11 Because they rebelled against the⌐words of⌐God *
    and despised the⌐counsel of the⌐Möst⌐High.

12 So he humbled their spirits with⌐härd⌐labor; *
    they stumbled, and⌐there was⌐none to⌐help.

13 Then they cried to the⌐LORD in their⌐trouble, *
    and he de⌐livered them from⌐their dis⌐tress.

14 He led them out of darkness and⌐dëep⌐gloom *
    and⌐broke their⌐bonds a⌐sunder.

248

William Crotch

251

Thomas Attwood

15 Let them give thanks to the ¦ LORD for his ¦ mercy *
   and the ¦ wonders he ¦ does for his ¦ children.

16 For he shatters the ¦ doors of ¦ bronze *
   and breaks in ¦ two the ¦ iron ¦ bars.

247   *William Savage*   **250**   *John Blow*

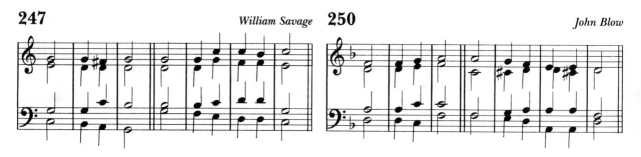

17 Some were fools and took to re ¦ bellious ¦ ways; *
   they were af ¦ flicted be ¦ cause of their ¦ sins.

18 They abhorred all ¦ manner of ¦ food *
   and drew ¦ near to ¦ deäth's ¦ door.

19 Then they cried to the ¦ LORD in their ¦ trouble, *
   and he de ¦ livered them from ¦ their dis ¦ tress.

20 He sent forth his ¦ word and ¦ healed them *
   and ¦ saved them ¦ from the ¦ grave.

248 *William Crotch*

251 *Thomas Attwood*

21 Let them give thanks to the⸍LORD for his⸍mercy *
   and the⸍wonders he⸍does for his⸍children.

22 Let them offer a⸍sacrifice of⸍thanksgiving *
   and tell of his⸍acts with⸍shouts of⸍joy.

247 *William Savage* **250** *John Blow*

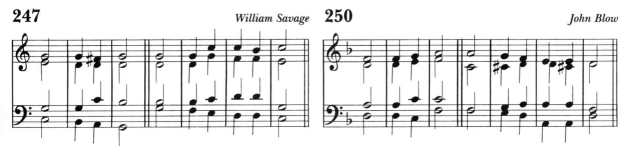

23 Some went down to the⸍sea in⸍ships *
   and plied their⸍trade in⸍dëep⸍waters;

24 They beheld the⸍works of the⸍LORD *
   and his⸍wonders⸍in the⸍deep.

25 Then he spoke, and a stormy⸍wind a⸍rose, *
   which tossed⸍high the⸍waves of the⸍sea.

26 They mounted up to the heavens and fell⸍back to the⸍depths; *
   their hearts⸍melted be⸍cause of their⸍peril.

247   *William Savage*   **250**   *John Blow*

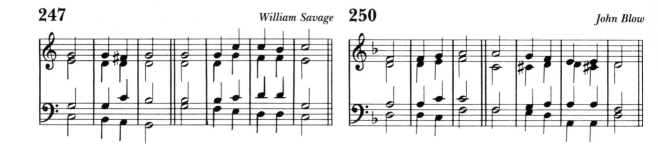

27 They reeled and 'staggered like 'drunkards *
   and were 'at their 'wits' 'end.

28 Then they cried to the 'LORD in their 'trouble, *
   and he de'livered them from 'their dis'tress.

29 He stilled the 'storm to a 'whisper *
   and 'quieted the 'waves of the 'sea.

30 Then were they glad be'cause of the 'calm, *
   and he brought them to the 'harbor 'they were 'bound for.

248   *William Crotch*

251   *Thomas Attwood*

31 Let them give thanks to the 'LORD for his 'mercy *
   and the 'wonders he 'does for his 'children.

32 Let them exalt him in the congre'gation of the 'people *
   and 'praise him in the 'council of the 'elders.

Psalm 107: Part 2 *Posuit flumina*

246 *Jonathan Battishill* **249** *Ray Francis Brown*

33 The LORD changed ͡rivers in͡to ͐deserts, *
   and water-springs ͐into ͐thirsty ͐ground,

34 A fruitful ͐land i͡nto ͐salt flats, *
   because of the ͡wickedness of ͐those who ͐dwell there.

35 He changed deserts into ͐pools of ͐water *
   and ͐dry land ͐into ͐water-springs.

36 He settled the ͐hungry ͐there, *
   and they ͡founded a ͡city to ͐dwell in.

37 They sowed fields, and ͐planted ͐vineyards, *
   and brought ͐in a ͐fruitful ͐harvest.

38 He blessed them, so that they ͐increased ͐greatly; *
   he did not ͐let their ͐herds de ͐crease.

39 Yet when they were diminished and ͡brought ͐low, *
   through ͡stress of ad ͐versity and ͐sorrow,

40 (He pours con ͐tempt on ͐princes *
   and makes them ͡wander in ͐trackless ͐wastes)

41 He lifted up the ͐poor o͡ut of ͐misery *
   and multiplied their ͐fam͡ilies like ͐flocks of ͐sheep.

42 The upright will ͡see this and re ͐joice, *
   but all ͡wickedness will ͐shut its ͐mouth.

43 Whoever is wise will ͡ponder these ͐things, *
   and consider well the ͐mercies ͐of the LORD.

When required, Gloria Patri may be sung to #248 in setting 1; to #251 in setting 2.

245

Psalm 108   *Paratum cor meum*

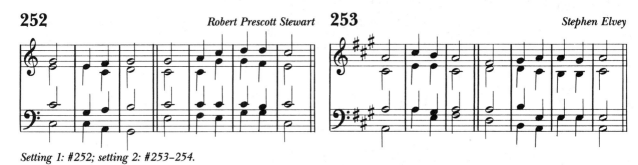

252   *Robert Prescott Stewart*   **253**   *Stephen Elvey*

Setting 1: #252; setting 2: #253–254.

1 My heart is firmly fixed, O God, my ˈheart is ˈfixed; *
    I will ˈsing and ˈmäke ˈmelody.

2 Wake up, my spirit;
    awake, ˈlute and ˈharp; *
        I myˈself will ˈwaken the ˈdawn.

3 I will confess you among the ˈpeoples, O ˈLORD; *
    I will sing praises to ˈyou aˈmong the ˈnations.

4 For your loving-kindness is ˈgreater than the ˈheavens, *
    and your faithfulness ˈreaches ˈto the ˈclouds.

5 Exalt yourself above the ˈheavens, O ˈGod, *
    and your ˈglory over ˈall the ˈearth.

6 So that those who are dear to you may ˈbe deˈlivered, *
    save with your ˈright ˈhand and ˈanswer me.

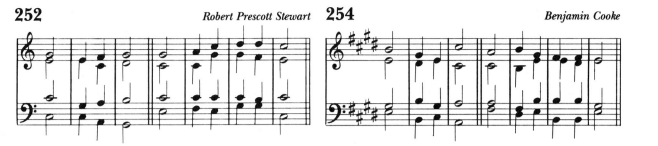

7 God spoke from his holy ' place and ' said, *
> "I will exult and parcel out Shechem;
> I will di ' vide the ' valley of ' Succoth.

8 Gilead is mine and Ma ' nasseh is ' mine; *
> Ephraim is my ' helmet and ' Judah my ' scepter.

9 Moab is my washbasin,
> on Edom I throw down my ' sandal to ' claim it, *
> and over Philistia ' will I ' shout in ' triumph."

10 Who will lead me into the ' strong ' city? *
> who will ' bring me ' into ' Edom?

11 Have you not cast us ' off, O ' God? *
> you no longer go ' out, O ' God, with our ' armies.

12 Grant us your help a ' gainst the ' enemy, *
> for ' vain is the ' help of ' man.

13 With God we will do ' valiant ' deeds, *
> and he shall tread our ' enemies ' under ' foot.

Psalm 109   *Deus, laudem*

255

William Morley

257

William Bayley

Setting 1: #255–256; setting 2: #257–258.

1 Hold not your tongue, O ˈGod of my ˈpraise; *
   for the mouth of the wicked,
   the mouth of the de ˈceitful, is ˈopened a ˈgainst me.

2 They speak to me with a ˈlying ˈtongue; *
   they encompass me with hateful words
   and fight a ˈgainst me with ˈout a ˈcause.

3 Despite my ˈlove, they ac ˈcuse me; *
   but ˈas for ˈme, I ˈpray for them.

4 They repay ˈevil for ˈgood, *
   and ˈhatred ˈfor my ˈlove.

5 Set a wicked ˈman a ˈgainst him, *
   and let an accuser ˈstand at ˈhis right ˈhand.

6 When he is judged, let him be ˈfoünd ˈguilty, *
   and ˈlet his ap ˈpeal be in ˈvain.

7 Let his ˈdays be ˈfew, *
   and let an ˈother ˈtake his ˈoffice.

8 Let his ˈchildren be ˈfatherless, *
   and his ˈwife be ˈcome a ˈwidow.

9 Let his children be'waifs and'beggars; *

    let them be driven from the'ruins'of their'homes.

10 Let the creditor seize'everything he'has; *

    let'strangers'plunder his'gains.

11 Let there be no one to'show him'kindness, *

    and none to'pity his'fatherless'children.

12 Let his des'cendants be de'stroyed, *

    and his name be blotted'out in the'next gene'ration.

13 Let the wickedness of his fathers be remembered be'fore the'LORD, *

    and his mother's sin'not be'blotted'out;

14 Let their sin be always be'fore the'LORD; *

    but let him root'out their'names from the'earth;

15 Because he did not remember to'shŏw'mercy, *

    but persecuted the poor and needy

    and sought to'kill the'broken'hearted.

16 He loved cursing,

    let it'come up'on him; *

    he took no delight in'blessing,'

    let it de'part from him.

17 He put on'cursing like a'garment, *

    let it soak into his body like water

    and'into his'bones like'oil;

18 Let it be to him like the cloak which he wraps a'round him'self, *

    and like the'belt that he'wears con'tinually.

†19 Let this be the recompense from the LORD to'my ac'cusers, *

    and to'those who speak'evil a'gainst me.

Tune change

256

William Morley

258

John Goss

20 But you, O Lord my GOD,
    oh, deal with me ac'cording to your'Name; *
    for your tender'mercy's'sake, de'liver me.

21 For I am'poor and'needy, *
    and my'heart is'wounded with'in me.

22 I have faded away like a'shadow when it'lengthens; *
    I am'shaken off'like a'locust.

23 My knees are'weak through'fasting, *
    and my'flesh is'wasted and'gaunt.

†24 I have be'come a re'proach to them; *
    they'see and'shake their'heads.

25 Help me, O'LORD my'God; *
    —'save me for your'mercy's'sake.

26 Let them know that'this is your'hand, *
    that'you, O'LORD, have'done it.

27 They may curse, but'you will'bless; *
    let those who rise up against me be put to shame,
    and your'servant'will re'joice.

28 Let my accusers be'clothed with dis'grace *
    and wrap themselves in their'shame as'in a'cloak.

29 I will give great thanks to the 'LORD with my 'mouth; *
in the midst of the 'multitude 'will I 'praise him;

30 Because he stands at the right 'hand of the 'needy, *
to save his life from 'those who 'would con 'demn him.

Psalm 110   *Dixit Dominus*

259   *Edwin George Monk*

260   *Ned Rorem*

1 The LORD said to my Lord, "Sit at 'my right 'hand, *
until I 'make your 'enemies your 'footstool."

2 The LORD will send the scepter of your 'power out of 'Zion, *
saying, "Rule over your 'enemies 'round a 'bout you.

†3 Princely state has been yours from the 'day of your 'birth; *
in the beauty of holiness have I begotten you,
like 'dew from the 'womb of the 'morning."

4 The LORD has sworn and he will 'not re 'cant: *
"You are a priest for ever after the 'order 'of Mel 'chizedek."

5 The Lord who is at your right hand
will smite kings in the 'day of his 'wrath; *
he will 'rule 'over the 'nations.

6 He will heap 'high the 'corpses; *
he will smash heads 'over the 'wide 'earth.

7 He will drink from the brook be 'side the 'road; *
therefore 'he will lift 'high his 'head.

251

Psalm 111   *Confitebor tibi*

261   *Richard Massey*

262   *Daniel Pinkham*

1 Hallelujah!
  I will give thanks to the LORD with my 'whöle 'heart, *
  in the assembly of the upright, 'in the 'congre 'gation.

2 Great are the 'deeds of the 'LORD! *
  they are 'studied by 'all who de 'light in them.

3 His work is full of 'majesty and 'splendor, *
  and his 'righteousness en 'dures for 'ever.

4 He makes his marvelous works to 'be re 'membered; *
  the LORD is 'gracious and 'full of com 'passion.

5 He gives food to 'those who 'fear him; *
  he is ever 'mindful 'of his 'covenant.

6 He has shown his people the 'power of his 'works *
  in 'giving them the 'lands of the 'nations.

7 The works of his hands are 'faithfulness and 'justice; *
  — 'all his com 'mandments are 'sure.

8 They stand fast for 'ever and 'ever, *
  because they are 'done in 'truth and 'equity.

9 He sent redemption to his people;
  he commanded his'covenant for'ever; *
    holy and'awesome'is his'Name.

10 The fear of the LORD is the be'ginning of'wisdom; *
    those who act accordingly have a good understanding;
    his'praise en'dures for'ever.

Psalm 112 *Beatus vir*

263

David Hurd

264

Thomas Attwood

1 Hallelujah!
  Happy are they who'fear the'LORD *
    and have great de'light in'his com'mandments!

2 Their descendants will be'mighty in the'land; *
    the generation of the'upright'will be'blessed.

3 Wealth and riches will'be in their'house, *
    and their'righteousness will'last for'ever.

4 Light shines in the'darkness for the'upright; *
    the righteous are'merciful and'full of com'passion.

5 It is good for them to be'generous in'lending *
    and to'manage their af'fairs with'justice.

6 For they will'never be'shaken; *
    the righteous will be kept in'ever'lasting re'membrance.

253

263

David Hurd

264

Thomas Attwood

7 They will not be afraid of any'evil'rumors; *
    their heart is right;
    they'put their'trust in the'Lord.

8 Their heart is established and'will not'shrink, *
    until they see their de'sire up'on their'enemies.

9 They have given'freely to the'poor, *
    and their righteousness stands fast for ever;
    they will'hold up their'head with'honor.

10 The wicked will see it and be angry;
    they will gnash their teeth and'pine a'way; *
    the de'sires of the'wicked will'perish.

Psalm 113 *Laudate, pueri*

265 *Ray Francis Brown*

266 *James Turle*

1 Hallelujah!
  Give praise, you⎡servants of the⎤LORD; *
  —⎡praise the⎤Name of the⎤LORD.

2 Let the Name of the⎤LORD be⎤blessed, *
  from this time⎤forth for⎤ever⎤more.

3 From the rising of the sun to its⎤going⎤down *
  let the⎤Name of the⎤LORD be⎤praised.

4 The LORD is high above⎤all⎤nations, *
  and his⎤glory a⎤bove the⎤heavens.

5 Who is like the LORD our God, who sits en⎤throned on⎤high, *
  but stoops to be⎤hold the⎤heavens and the⎤earth?

6 He takes up the weak⎤out of the⎤dust *
  and lifts up the⎤poor⎤from the⎤ashes.

7 He⎤sets them with the⎤princes, *
  with the⎤princes⎤of his⎤people.

8 He makes the woman of a⎤childless⎤house *
  to be a⎤joyful⎤mother of⎤children.

Psalm 114   *In exitu Israel*

267   *David Hurd (after Peregrinus)*

268   *George Mursell Garrett*

1 Hallelujah!
   When Israel came 'out of 'Egypt, *
      the house of Jacob from a 'people of 'strange 'speech,

2 Judah be'came God's 'sanctuary *
      and 'Israel 'his do'minion.

3 The sea be'held it and 'fled; *
      Jordan 'turned and 'went 'back.

4 The mountains 'skipped like 'rams, *
      and the little 'hills like 'young 'sheep.

5 What ailed you, O 'sea, that you 'fled? *
      O 'Jordan, that 'you turned 'back?

6 You mountains, that you 'skipped like 'rams? *
      you little 'hills like 'young 'sheep?

7 Tremble, O earth, at the 'presence of the 'Lord, *
      at the 'presence of the 'God of 'Jacob,

8 Who turned the hard rock into a 'pool of 'water *
      and flint-stone 'into a 'flowing 'spring.

256

Psalm 115 *Non nobis, Domine*

269   *Sydney Nicholson*

270   *Gerald Knight*

1 Not to us, O LORD, not to us,
   but to your⎸Name give⎸glory; *
      because of your⎸love and be⎸cause of your⎸faithfulness.

2 Why should the⎸heathen⎸say, *
      —⎸"Where then⎸is their⎸God?"

3 Our⎸God is in⎸heaven; *
      whatever he⎸wills to⎸do he⎸does.

4 Their idols are⎸silver and⎸gold, *
      the⎸work of⎸human⎸hands.

5 They have mouths, but they⎸cannot⎸speak; *
      eyes have they,⎸but they⎸cannot⎸see;

6 They have ears, but they⎸cannot⎸hear; *
      noses,⎸but they⎸cannot⎸smell;

7 They have hands, but they cannot feel;
   feet, but they⎸cannot⎸walk; *
      they make no⎸soünd⎸with their⎸throat.

8 Those who⎸make them are⎸like them, *
      and so are⎸all who⎸put their⎸trust in them.

257

269

Sydney Nicholson

270

Gerald Knight

9 O Israel, 'trust in the 'LORD; *
   he is their 'hëlp 'and their 'shield.

10 O house of Aaron, 'trust in the 'LORD, *
   he is their 'hëlp 'and their 'shield.

11 You who fear the LORD, 'trust in the 'LORD; *
   he is their 'hëlp 'and their 'shield.

12 The LORD has been mindful of us, and 'he will 'bless us; *
   he will bless the house of Israel;
   he will 'bless the 'house of 'Aaron;

13 He will bless those who 'fear the 'LORD, *
   both 'small and 'great to 'gether.

14 May the LORD increase you 'more and 'more, *
   — 'you and your 'children 'after you.

15 May you be 'blessed by the 'LORD, *
   the 'maker of 'heaven and 'earth.

16 The heaven of 'heavens is the 'LORD's, *
   but he en 'trusted the 'earth to its 'peoples.

17 The dead do not 'praise the 'LORD, *
   nor all 'those who go 'down into 'silence;

18 But we will 'bless the 'LORD, *
   from this time forth for ever 'möre. '
   'Halle 'lujah!

Psalm 116 *Dilexi, quoniam*

271

William Crotch

272

Percy Buck

Reproduced by permission of Novello and Company, Ltd.

1 I love the LORD, because he has heard the voice of my'suppli'cation, *
  because he has inclined his ear to me when'ever I'called up'on him.

2 The cords of death entangled me;
  the grip of the'grave took'hold of me; *
  I'came to'grief and'sorrow.

†3 Then I called upon the'Name of the'LORD: *
  "O LORD, I'pray you,'save my'life."

4 Gracious is the'LORD and'righteous; *
  our'God is'full of com'passion.

5 The LORD watches'over the'innocent; *
  I was brought very'löw,'and he'helped me.

6 Turn again to your rest,'O my'soul, *
  for the'LORD has'treated you'well.

7 For you have rescued my'life from'death, *
  my eyes from'tears, and my'feet from'stumbling.

8 I will walk in the'presence of the'LORD *
  —'in the'land of the'living.

271   *William Crotch*

272   *Percy Buck*

9 I believed, even when I said,
    "I have been 'brought very 'low." *
       In my distress I said, '"No one 'can be 'trusted."

10 How shall I re'pay the 'LORD *
       for all the 'good things 'he has 'done for me?

11 I will lift up the 'cup of sal'vation *
       and 'call upon the 'Name of the 'LORD.

12 I will fulfill my 'vows to the 'LORD *
       in the 'presence of 'all his 'people.

13 Precious in the 'sight of the 'LORD *
       is the 'death 'of his 'servants.

14 O LORD, 'I am your 'servant; *
       I am your servant and the child of your handmaid;
       you have 'freed me 'from my 'bonds.

15 I will offer you the 'sacrifice of 'thanksgiving *
       and 'call upon the 'Name of the 'LORD.

16 I will fulfill my 'vows to the 'LORD *
       in the 'presence of 'all his 'people,

17 In the 'courts of the 'LORD's house, *
       in the midst of you, O Je'rusalem. '
       Halle'lujah!

Psalm 117   *Laudate Dominum*

273   *John Stainer*   **274**   *Philip Tordoff*

1 Praise the LORD, ⎸all you ⎸nations; *
   —⎸laud him, ⎸all you ⎸peoples.

2 For his loving-kindness ⎸toward us is ⎸great, *
   and the faithfulness of the LORD endures for ⎸ever. ⎸
   Halle⎸lujah!

Psalm 118   *Confitemini Domino*

275   *George Elvey*

276   *George Thalben-Ball*

1 Give thanks to the LORD, for ⎸he is ⎸good; *
   his ⎸mercy en⎸dures for ⎸ever.

2 Let Israel ⎸now pro⎸claim, *
   "His ⎸mercy en⎸dures for ⎸ever."

3 Let the house of Aaron ⎸now pro⎸claim, *
   "His ⎸mercy en⎸dures for ⎸ever."

4 Let those who fear the LORD ⎸now pro⎸claim, *
   "His ⎸mercy en⎸dures for ⎸ever."

275

George Elvey

276

George Thalben-Ball

5 I called to the LORD in⎜my dis⎜tress; *
  the LORD⎜answered by⎜setting me⎜free.

6 The LORD is at my side, therefore I⎜will not⎜fear; *
  —⎜what can⎜anyone⎜do to me?

†7 The LORD is at my⎜side to⎜help me; *
  I will⎜triumph over⎜those who⎜hate me.

8 It is better to re⎜ly on the⎜LORD *
  than to⎜put any⎜trust in⎜flesh.

9 It is better to re⎜ly on the⎜LORD *
  than to⎜put any⎜trust in⎜rulers.

10 All the un⎜godly en⎜compass me; *
  in the name of the⎜LORD I⎜will re⎜pel them.

11 They hem me in, they hem me in on⎜every⎜side; *
  in the name of the⎜LORD I⎜will re⎜pel them.

12 They swarm about me like bees;
  they blaze like a⎜fire of⎜thorns; *
  in the name of the⎜LORD I⎜will re⎜pel them.

13 I was pressed so hard that I⎜almost⎜fell, *
  but the⎜LÖRD⎜came to my⎜help.

14 The LORD is my⎜strength and my⎜song, *
  and he has be⎜cöme⎜my sal⎜vation.

15 There is a sound of exul'tation and 'victory *
—'in the 'tents of the 'righteous:

†16 "The right hand of the 'LORD has 'triumphed! *
the right hand of the LORD is exalted!
the right 'hand of the 'LORD has 'triumphed!"

17 I shall not 'die, but 'live, *
and de'clare the 'works of the 'LORD.

18 The LORD has 'punished me 'sorely, *
but he did not 'hand me 'over to 'death.

19 Open for me the 'gates of 'righteousness; *
I will enter them;
I will 'offer 'thanks to the 'LORD.

20 "This is the 'gate of the 'LORD; *
—'he who is 'righteous may 'enter."

21 I will give thanks to you, 'for you 'answered me *
and have be'come 'my sal'vation.

22 The same stone which the 'builders re'jected *
has be'come the 'chief 'cornerstone.

23 This is the 'LORD's 'doing, *
and it is 'marvelous 'in our 'eyes.

24 On this day the 'LORD has 'acted; *
we will re'joïce 'and be 'glad in it.

25 Hosanna, 'LORD, ho'sanna! *
LORD, 'send us 'now suc'cess.

26 Blessed is he who comes in the 'name of the 'Lord; *
we 'bless you from the 'house of the 'LORD.

†27 God is the LORD; he has 'shined up'on us; *
form a procession with branches 'up to the 'horns of the 'altar.

28 "You are my God, and 'I will 'thank you; *
you are my 'God, and 'I will ex'alt you."

29 Give thanks to the LORD, for 'he is 'good; *
his 'mercy en'dures for 'ever.

Psalm 119: Aleph   *Beati immaculati*

277
James Nares

290
Edward John Hopkins

Setting 1: #277–289; setting 2: #290–299.

1 Happy are those whose ˈway is ˈblameless, *
  who ˈwalk in the ˈlaw of the ˈLORD!

2 Happy are they who obˈserve his deˈcrees *
  and ˈseek him with ˈall their ˈhearts!

3 Who never do ˈany ˈwrong, *
  but ˈalways ˈwalk in his ˈways.

4 You laid ˈdown your comˈmandments, *
  that ˈwe should ˈfully ˈkeep them.

5 Oh, that my ways were ˈmade so diˈrect *
  that ˈI might ˈkeep your ˈstatutes!

6 Then I should not be ˈput to ˈshame, *
  when I reˈgard all ˈyour comˈmandments.

7 I will thank you with an ˈunfeigned ˈheart, *
  when I have ˈlearned your ˈrighteous ˈjudgments.

8 I will ˈkeep your ˈstatutes; *
  —ˈdo not ˈutterly forˈsake me.

Psalm 119: Beth *In quo corrigit?*

278 Frederick A. Gore Ouseley

290 Edward John Hopkins

9 How shall a young man ' cleanse his ' way? *
   By ' keeping ' to your ' words.

10 With my whole ' heart I ' seek you; *
   let me not ' stray from ' your com ' mandments.

11 I treasure your ' promise in my ' heart, *
   that I ' may not ' sin a ' gainst you.

12 Blessèd are ' you, O ' LORD; *
   in ' struct me ' in your ' statutes.

13 With my ' lips will I re ' cite *
   all the ' judgments ' of your ' mouth.

14 I have taken greater delight in the ' way of your de ' crees *
   than in ' all ' manner of ' riches.

15 I will meditate on ' your com ' mandments *
   and give at ' tention ' to your ' ways.

16 My delight is ' in your ' statutes; *
   I will ' not for ' get your ' word.

Psalm 119: Gimel   *Retribue servo tuo*

277   *James Nares*

291   *Gilbert Heathcote*

17 Deal bountifully ǀ with your ǀ servant, *
     that I may ǀ live and ǀ keep your ǀ word.

18 Open my eyes, that ǀ I may ǀ see *
     the ǀ wonders ǀ of your ǀ law.

19 I am a stranger ǀ here on ǀ earth; *
     do not ǀ hide your com ǀ mandments ǀ from me.

20 My soul is consumed at ǀ äll ǀ times *
     with ǀ longing ǀ for your ǀ judgments.

21 You have re ǀ buked the ǀ insolent; *
     cursed are they who ǀ stray from ǀ your com ǀ mandments!

22 Turn from me ǀ shame and re ǀ buke, *
     for ǀ I have ǀ kept your de ǀ crees.

23 Even though rulers sit and ǀ plot a ǀ gainst me, *
     I will ǀ meditate ǀ on your ǀ statutes.

24 For your decrees are ǀ my de ǀ light, *
     — ǀ and they ǀ are my ǀ counselors.

Psalm 119: Daleth   *Adhaesit pavimento*

279   *John Blow*

291   *Gilbert Heathcote*

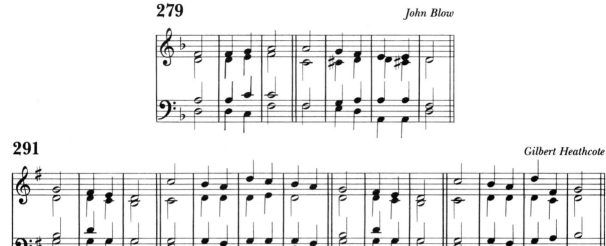

25 My soul'cleaves to the'dust; *
    give me life ac'cording'to your'word.

26 I have confessed my'ways, and you'answered me; *
    in'struct me'in your'statutes.

27 Make me understand the'way of your com'mandments, *
    that I may meditate'on your'marvelous'works.

28 My soul melts a'way for'sorrow; *
    strengthen me ac'cording'to your'word.

29 Take from me the'way of'lying; *
    let me find'gräce'through your'law.

30 I have chosen the'way of'faithfulness; *
    I have'set your'judgments be'fore me.

31 I hold'fast to your de'crees; *
    O LORD, let me'not be'put to'shame.

32 I will run the'way of your com'mandments, *
    for you have'set my'heart at'liberty.

Psalm 119: He
Legem pone

280 *Stephen Elvey*

292 *John Jones*

33 Teach me, O LORD, the 'way of your 'statutes, *
    and I shall 'keep it 'to the 'end.

34 Give me understanding, and I shall 'keep your 'law; *
    I shall 'keep it with 'all my 'heart.

35 Make me go in the 'path of your com'mandments, *
    for 'that is 'my de'sire.

36 Incline my 'heart to your de'crees *
    and 'not to 'unjust 'gain.

37 Turn my eyes from 'watching what is 'worthless; *
    give me 'life 'in your 'ways.

38 Fulfill your 'promise to your 'servant, *
    which you 'make to 'those who 'fear you.

39 Turn away the re'proach which I 'dread, *
    be'cause your 'judgments are 'good.

40 Behold, I 'long for your com'mandments; *
    in your 'righteousness pre'serve my 'life.

Psalm 119: Waw   *Et veniat super me*

281   *John Goss*

292   *John Jones*

41 Let your loving-kindness ˈcome to me, Oˈ LORD, *
   and your salvation, acˈcordingˈ to yourˈ promise.

42 Then shall I have a word forˈ those whoˈ taunt me, *
   beˈcause Iˈ trust in yourˈ words.

43 Do not take the word of truthˈ out of myˈ mouth, *
   for myˈ hope isˈ in yourˈ judgments.

44 I shall continue toˈ keep yourˈ law; *
   I shallˈ keep it forˈ ever andˈ ever.

45 I willˈ walk atˈ liberty, *
   because Iˈ studyˈ your comˈmandments.

46 I will tell of your deˈcrees beforeˈ kings *
   andˈ will notˈ be aˈshamed.

47 I deˈlight in your comˈmandments, *
   whichˈ I haveˈ alwaysˈ loved.

48 I will lift up myˈ hands to your comˈmandments, *
   and I willˈ meditateˈ on yourˈ statutes.

Psalm 119: Zayin *Memor esto verbi tui*

280   *Stephen Elvey*

293   *Stephen Elvey*

49 Remember your⌐word⌐to your⌐servant, *
       because⌐you have⌐given me⌐hope.

50 This is my⌐comfort in my⌐trouble, *
       that your⌐promise⌐gives me⌐life.

51 The proud have de⌐rided me⌐cruelly, *
       but⌐I have not⌐turned from your⌐law.

52 When I remember your⌐judgments of⌐old, *
       O⌐LORD, I⌐take great⌐comfort.

53 I am filled with a⌐burning⌐rage, *
       because of the⌐wicked who for⌐sake your law.

54 Your statutes have⌐been like⌐songs to me *
       wherever⌐I have⌐lived as a⌐stranger.

55 I remember your Name in the⌐night, O⌐LORD, *
       and⌐dwell up⌐on your⌐law.

56 This is⌐how it has⌐been with me, *
       because⌐I have⌐kept your com⌐mandments.

Psalm 119: Heth *Portio mea, Domine*

282 *C. Hylton Stewart*

293 *Stephen Elvey*

57 You only are my ⌐portion, O ˈLORD; *
  I have ˈpromised to ˈkeep your ˈwords.

58 I entreat you with ˈall my ˈheart, *
  be merciful to me ac ˈcording ˈto your ˈpromise.

59 I have con ˈsidered my ˈways *
  and turned my ˈfeet toward ˈyour de ˈcrees.

60 I hasten and ˈdo not ˈtarry *
  to ˈkëep ˈyour com ˈmandments.

61 Though the cords of the ˈwicked en ˈtangle me, *
  I do ˈnot for ˈget your ˈlaw.

62 At midnight I will rise to ˈgive you ˈthanks, *
  be ˈcause of your ˈrighteous ˈjudgments.

63 I am a companion of ˈall who ˈfear you *
  and of ˈthose who ˈkeep your com ˈmandments.

64 The earth, O LORD, is ˈfull of your ˈlove; *
  in ˈstruct me ˈin your ˈstatutes.

Psalm 119: Teth   *Bonitatem fecisti*

280   *Stephen Elvey*

293   *Stephen Elvey*

65 O Lord, you have dealt graciously'with your'servant, *
  ac'cording'to your'word.

66 Teach me dis'cernment and'knowledge, *
  for I have be'lieved in'your com'mandments.

67 Before I was afflicted I'went a'stray, *
  but'now I'keep your'word.

68 You are good and you'bring forth'good; *
  in'struct me'in your'statutes.

69 The proud have'smeared me with'lies, *
  but I will keep your com'mandments with my'whöle'heart.

70 Their heart is'gross and'fat, *
  but my de'light is'in your'law.

71 It is good for me that'I have been af'flicted, *
  that'I might'learn your'statutes.

72 The law of your mouth is'dearer to'me *
  than'thousands in'gold and'silver.

Psalm 119: Yodh *Manus tuae fecerunt me*

283

Parisian Tone

294

George Elvey

73 Your hands have ˈmade me and ˈfashioned me; *
    give me understanding, that I may ˈleärn ˈyour comˈmandments.

74 Those who fear you will be ˈglad when they ˈsee me, *
    beˈcause I ˈtrust in your ˈword.

75 I know, O LORD, that your ˈjudgments are ˈright *
    and that in ˈfaithfulness ˈyou have afˈflicted me.

76 Let your lovingˈkindness be my ˈcomfort, *
    as you have ˈpromised ˈto your ˈservant.

77 Let your compassion come to me, that ˈI may ˈlive, *
    for your ˈlaw is ˈmy deˈlight.

78 Let the arrogant be put to shame, for they ˈwrong me with ˈlies; *
    but I will ˈmeditate on ˈyour comˈmandments.

79 Let those who ˈfear you ˈturn to me, *
    and also ˈthose who ˈknow your deˈcrees.

80 Let my heart be ˈsound in your ˈstatutes, *
    that I may ˈnot be ˈput to ˈshame.

Psalm 119: Kaph
Defecit in salutare

284

Edwin George Monk

294

George Elvey

81 My soul has ˈlonged for your salˈvation; *
    I have ˈput my ˈhope in your ˈword.

82 My eyes have failed from ˈwatching for your ˈpromise, *
    and I ˈsäy, ˈ"When will you ˈcomfort me?"

83 I have become like a leather ˈflask in the ˈsmoke, *
    but I have ˈnot for ˈgotten your ˈstatutes.

84 How much ˈlonger must I ˈwait? *
    when will you give ˈjudgment against ˈthose who ˈpersecute me?

85 The ˈproud have dug ˈpits for me; *
    they ˈdo not ˈkeep your ˈlaw.

86 All your com ˈmandments are ˈtrue; *
    help me, for they ˈpersecute ˈme with ˈlies.

87 They had almost made an ˈend of me on ˈearth, *
    but I have not for ˈsaken ˈyour com ˈmandments.

88 In your loving ˈkindness, re ˈvive me, *
    that I may ˈkeep the de ˈcrees of your ˈmouth.

Psalm 119: Lamedh   *In aeternum, Domine*

285   R.H. Stanley

295   William Crotch

89 O LORD, your word is ' ever ' lasting; *
    it ' stands ' firm in the ' heavens.

90 Your faithfulness remains from one gene ' ration to an ' other; *
    you established the ' earth, and ' it a ' bides.

91 By your decree these con ' tinue to this ' day, *
    for ' all things ' are your ' servants.

92 If my delight had not ' been in your ' law, *
    I should have ' perished in ' my af ' fliction.

93 I will never for ' get your com ' mandments, *
    because by ' them you ' give me ' life.

94 I am yours; oh, that ' you would ' save me! *
    for I ' study ' your com ' mandments.

95 Though the wicked lie in wait for me ' to des ' troy me, *
    I will apply my ' mind to ' your de ' crees.

96 I see that all things ' come to an ' end, *
    but your com ' mandment ' has no ' bounds.

Psalm 119: Mem
Quomodo dilexi!

283

Parisian Tone

295

William Crotch

97 Oh, how I ˈlove your ˈlaw! *
    all the day ˈlong it isˈin my ˈmind.

98 Your commandment has made me ˈwiser than my ˈenemies, *
    and ˈit is ˈalways ˈwith me.

99 I have more understanding than ˈall my ˈteachers, *
    for ˈyour de ˈcrees are my ˈstudy.

100 I am ˈwiser than the ˈelders, *
    because ˈI ob ˈserve your com ˈmandments.

101 I restrain my feet from every ˈevil ˈway, *
    that ˈI may ˈkeep your ˈword.

102 I do not ˈshrink from your ˈjudgments, *
    because ˈyou your ˈself have ˈtaught me.

103 How sweet are your ˈwords to my ˈtaste! *
    they are sweeter than ˈhoney ˈto my ˈmouth.

104 Through your commandments I ˈgain under ˈstanding; *
    therefore I hate ˈevery ˈlying ˈway.

Psalm 119: Nun   *Lucerna pedibus meis*

286   *Edward Rimbault*

296   *R.P. Goodenough*

105 Your word is a'lantern to my'feet *
   and a'light up'on my'path.

106 I have'sworn and am de'termined *
   to'keep your'righteous'judgments.

107 I am'deeply'troubled; *
   preserve my life, O LORD, ac'cording'to your'word.

108 Accept, O LORD, the willing'tribute of my'lips, *
   and'teäch'me your'judgments.

109 My life is'always in my'hand, *
   yet I do'not for'get your'law.

110 The wicked have'set a'trap for me, *
   but I have not'strayed from'your com'mandments.

111 Your decrees are my in'heritance for'ever; *
   truly, they'are the'joy of my'heart.

112 I have applied my heart to ful'fill your'statutes *
   for'ever and'to the'end.

Psalm 119: Samekh   *Iniquos odio habui*

287   *Thomas Tallis*

296   *R.P. Goodenough*

113 I hate those who have a di'vided'heart, *
     but your'läw'do I'love.

114 You are my'refuge and'shield; *
     my'hope is'in your'word.

115 A'way from me, you'wicked! *
     I will keep the com'mandments'of my'God.

116 Sustain me according to your promise, that'I may'live, *
     and let me not be disap'pointed'in my'hope.

117 Hold me up, and'I shall be'safe, *
     and my delight shall be'ever'in your'statutes.

118 You spurn all who'stray from your'statutes; *
     their de'ceitfulness'is in'vain.

119 In your sight all the wicked of the'earth are but'dross; *
     —'therefore I'love your de'crees.

120 My flesh'trembles with'dread of you; *
     I am a'fräid'of your'judgments.

Psalm 119: Ayin   *Feci judicium*

286   Edward Rimbault

297   J. Soaper

121 I have done what is ˈjust and ˈright; *
   do not deˈliver me to ˈmy opˈpressors.

122 Be surety for your ˈservant's ˈgood; *
   let ˈnot the ˈproud opˈpress me.

123 My eyes have failed from watching for ˈyour salˈvation *
   and ˈfor your ˈrighteous ˈpromise.

124 Deal with your servant according to your ˈlovingˈkindness *
   and ˈteäch ˈme your ˈstatutes.

125 I am your servant; ˈgrant me underˈstanding, *
   that ˈI may ˈknow your deˈcrees.

126 It is time for you to ˈact, O ˈLORD, *
   for ˈthey have ˈbroken your ˈlaw.

127 Truly, I ˈlove your comˈmandments *
   more than ˈgold and ˈprecious ˈstones.

128 I hold all your comˈmandments to be ˈright for me; *
   all paths of ˈfalsehood ˈI abˈhor.

Psalm 119: Pe *Mirabilia*

285

R.H. Stanley

297

J. Soaper

129 Your de'crees are'wonderful; *
    therefore I o'bey them with'all my'heart.

130 When your word goes'forth it gives'light; *
    it gives under'standing'to the'simple.

131 I open my'mouth and'pant; *
    I'long for'your com'mandments.

132 Turn to'me in'mercy, *
    as you always do to'those who'love your'Name.

133 Steady my'footsteps in your'word; *
    let no iniquity'have do'minion'over me.

134 Rescue me from'those who op'press me, *
    and'I will'keep your com'mandments.

135 Let your countenance'shine upon your'servant *
    and'teäch'me your'statutes.

136 My eyes shed'streams of'tears, *
    because people'do not'keep your'law.

Psalm 119: Sadhe   *Justus es, Domine*

286   *Edward Rimbault*

297   *J. Soaper*

137 You are ⌐righteous, O ⌐LORD, *
     and ⌐upright ⌐are your ⌐judgments.

138 You have issued ⌐your de⌐crees *
     with ⌐justice and in ⌐perfect ⌐faithfulness.

139 My indig⌐nation has con⌐sumed me, *
     because my ⌐enemies for⌐get your ⌐words.

140 Your word has been ⌐tested to the ⌐uttermost, *
     and your ⌐servant ⌐holds it ⌐dear.

141 I am small and of ⌐little ac⌐count, *
     yet I do ⌐not for⌐get your com⌐mandments.

142 Your justice is an ever⌐lasting ⌐justice *
     and your ⌐läw ⌐is the ⌐truth.

143 Trouble and dis⌐tress have come up⌐on me, *
     yet your com⌐mandments are ⌐my de⌐light.

144 The righteousness of your decrees is ⌐ever⌐lasting; *
     grant me under⌐standing, that ⌐I may ⌐live.

Psalm 119: Qoph *Clamavi in toto corde meo*

288
Richard Farrant

298
Edward Higgins

145 I call with my ǀwhöleǀheart; *
  answer me, O LORD, thatǀI mayǀkeep yourǀstatutes.

146 I call to you;
  oh, thatǀyou wouldǀsave me! *
  —ǀI willǀkeep your deǀcrees.

147 Early in the morningǀI cryǀout to you, *
  for in yourǀwördǀis myǀtrust.

148 My eyes areǀopen in theǀnight watches, *
  that I mayǀmeditate upǀon yourǀpromise.

149 Hear my voice, O LORD, according to yourǀlovingǀkindness; *
  according to yourǀjudgments,ǀgive meǀlife.

150 They draw near who inǀmaliceǀpersecute me; *
  they areǀveryǀfar from yourǀlaw.

151 You, O LORD, areǀnear atǀhand, *
  andǀall your comǀmandments areǀtrue.

152 Long have Iǀknown from your deǀcrees *
  that you have esǀtablishedǀthem forǀever.

Psalm 119: Resh   *Vide humilitatem*

289
Edwin George Monk

298
Edward Higgins

153 Behold my af'fliction and de'liver me, *
   for I do'not for'get your'law.

154 Plead my'cause and re'deem me; *
   according to your'promise,'give me'life.

155 Deliverance is'far from the'wicked, *
   for they'do not'study your'statutes.

156 Great is your com'passion, O'LORD; *
   preserve my life, ac'cording'to your'judgments.

157 There are many who'persecute and op'press me, *
   yet I have not'swerved from'your de'crees.

158 I look with'loathing at the'faithless, *
   for'they have not'kept your'word.

159 See how I'love your com'mandments! *
   O'LORD, in your'mercy, pre'serve me.

160 The heart of your'word is'truth; *
   all your righteous judgments en'dure for'ever'more.

Psalm 119: Shin   *Principes persecuti sunt*

161 Rulers have persecuted me with'out a'cause, *
  but my heart'stands in'awe of your'word.

162 I am as glad be'cause of your'promise *
  as'one who'finds great'spoils.

163 As for lies, I'hate and ab'hor them, *
  but your'läw'is my'love.

164 Seven times a'day do I'praise you, *
  be'cause of your'righteous'judgments.

165 Great peace have they who'love your'law; *
  for'them there'is no'stumbling block.

166 I have hoped for your sal'vation, O'LORD, *
  and'I have ful'filled your com'mandments.

167 I have'kept your de'crees *
  and'I have'loved them'deeply.

168 I have kept your com'mandments and de'crees, *
  for'all my'ways are be'fore you.

Psalm 119: Taw   *Appropinquet deprecatio*

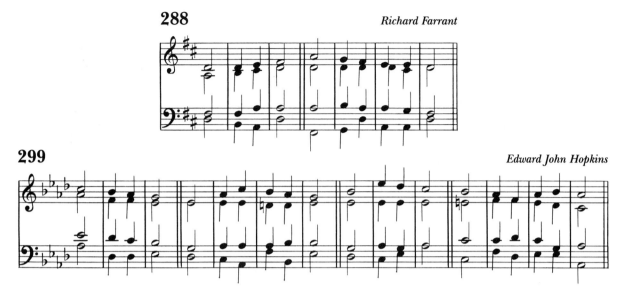

288   *Richard Farrant*

299   *Edward John Hopkins*

169 Let my cry come be'fore you, O 'LORD; *
  give me understanding, ac'cording 'to your 'word.

170 Let my suppli'cation come be'fore you; *
  deliver me, ac'cording 'to your 'promise.

171 My lips shall pour 'forth your 'praise, *
  —'when you 'teach me your 'statutes.

172 My tongue shall 'sing of your 'promise, *
  for 'all your com'mandments are 'righteous.

173 Let your hand be 'ready to 'help me, *
  for I have 'chosen 'your com'mandments.

174 I long for your sal'vation, O 'LORD, *
  and your 'law is 'my de'light.

175 Let me live, and 'I will 'praise you, *
  and 'let your 'judgments 'help me.

176 I have gone astray like a 'sheep that is 'lost; *
  search for your servant,
  for I do 'not for'get your com'mandments.

285

Psalm 120 *Ad Dominum*

300 *C. Hylton Stewart* **301** *Bryan Hesford*

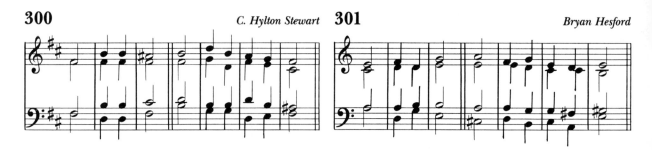

1 When I was in trouble, I'called to the'LORD; *
   I called to the'LORD,'and he'answered me.

2 Deliver me, O LORD, from'lying'lips *
   and'from the de'ceitful'tongue.

3 What shall be done to you, and what'more be'sides, *
   O'you de'ceitful'tongue?

4 The sharpened'arrows of a'warrior, *
   a'long with'hot glowing'coals.

5 How hateful it is that I must'lodge in'Meshech *
   and'dwell among the'tents of'Kedar!

6 Too long have I'had to'live *
   a'mong the'enemies of'peace.

7 I am on the'side of'peace, *
   but when I'speak of it,'they are for'war.

Psalm 121   *Levavi oculos*

302

Samuel Sebastian Wesley

303

Henry Walford Davies

1   I lift up my ' eyes to the ' hills; *
     from ' where is my ' help to ' come?

2   My help ' comes from the ' LORD, *
     the ' maker of ' heaven and ' earth.

3   He will not let your ' foot be ' moved *
     and he who watches over you ' will not ' fall a ' sleep.

4   Behold, he who keeps ' watch over ' Israel *
     shall ' neither ' slumber nor ' sleep;

5   The LORD himself ' watches ' over you; *
     the LORD is your ' shade at ' your right ' hand.

6   So that the sun shall not ' strike you by ' day, *
     — ' nor the ' moon by ' night.

7   The LORD shall preserve you from ' äll ' evil; *
     it is ' he who shall ' keep you ' safe.

8   The LORD shall watch over your going out and your ' coming ' in, *
     from this time ' forth for ' ever ' more.

287

Psalm 122   *Laetatus sum*

304   *David Hurd*

305   *Ivor Algernon Atkins*

1 I was glad when they ⸌said to ⸌me, *
    "Let us ⸌go to the ⸌house of the ⸌LORD."

2 Now our ⸌feet are ⸌standing *
    within your ⸌gätes, ⸌O Je⸌rusalem.

3 Jerusalem is ⸌built as a ⸌city *
    that is at ⸌unity ⸌with it⸌self;

4 To which the tribes go up,
    the ⸌tribes of the ⸌LORD, *
        the assembly of Israel,
    to ⸌praise the ⸌Name of the ⸌LORD.

†5 For there are the ⸌thrones of ⸌judgment, *
    the ⸌thrones of the ⸌house of ⸌David.

6 Pray for the ⸌peace of Je⸌rusalem: *
    — ⸌"May they ⸌prosper who ⸌love you.

7 Peace be with⸌in your ⸌walls *
    and ⸌quietness with⸌in your ⸌towers.

8 For my brethren and com⸌panions' ⸌sake, *
    I ⸌pray for ⸌your pros⸌perity.

9 Because of the house of the ⸌LORD our ⸌God, *
    I will ⸌seek to ⸌do you ⸌good."

Ad te levavi oculos meos

306 *C. Hylton Stewart* **307** *Henry Walford Davies*

1 To you I'lift up my'eyes, *
   to you en'throned'in the'heavens.

2 As the eyes of servants look to the'hand of their'masters, *
   and the eyes of a'maid to the'hand of her'mistress,

3 So our eyes look to the'LORD our'God, *
   un'til he'show us his'mercy.

4 Have mercy upon us, O'LORD, have'mercy, *
   for we have had'more than e'nough of con'tempt.

5 Too much of the scorn of the'indolent'rich, *
   and of the de'rision'of the'proud.

Psalm 124   *Nisi quia Dominus*

308

C. Hylton Stewart

309

Derrick Cantrell

1 If the LORD had not¹been on our¹side, *
   let¹Israel¹nöw¹say;

2 If the LORD had not¹been on our¹side, *
   when¹enemies rose¹up a¹gainst us;

3 Then would they have swallowed us¹up a¹live *
   in¹their fierce¹anger¹toward us;

4 Then would the waters have¹over¹whelmed us *
   —¹and the¹torrent gone¹over us;

5 Then would the¹raging¹waters *
   have¹göne¹right¹over us.

6 Blessèd¹be the¹LORD! *
   he has not given us over to be a¹prëy¹for their¹teeth.

7 We have escaped like a bird from the¹snare of the¹fowler; *
   the snare is¹broken, and¹we have es¹caped.

8 Our help is in the¹Name of the¹LORD, *
   the¹maker of¹heaven and¹earth.

Psalm 125 *Qui confidunt*

310 *Richard Farrant*   **311** *Peter Hurford*

1 Those who trust in the LORD are like ˈMoŭntˈZion, *
   which cannot beˈmoved, but standsˈfast forˈever.

2 The hills stand aˈbout Jeˈrusalem; *
   so does the LORD stand round about his people,
   from this timeˈforth forˈeverˈmore.

3 The scepter of the wicked shall not hold sway over the
            land alˈlotted to theˈjust, *
   so that the just shall notˈput theirˈhands toˈevil.

4 Show your goodness, O LORD, toˈthose who areˈgood *
   and toˈthose who areˈtrue ofˈheart.

5 As for those who turn aside to crooked ways,
   the LORD will lead them away with theˈevilˈdoers; *
   butˈpeace be upˈönˈIsrael.

Psalm 126 *In convertendo*

312

Edward Rimbault

313

Charles Villiers Stanford

1 When the LORD restored the 'fortunes of 'Zion, *
   then 'were we like 'those who 'dream.

2 Then was our mouth 'filled with 'laughter, *
   and our 'tongue with 'shouts of 'joy.

†3 Then they said a 'mong the 'nations, *
   "The 'LORD has done 'great things 'for them."

4 The LORD has done 'great things for 'us, *
   and 'we are 'glad in 'deed.

5 Restore our 'fortunes, O 'LORD, *
   like the 'watercourses 'of the 'Negev.

6 Those who 'sowed with 'tears *
   will 'reap with 'songs of 'joy.

7 Those who go out weeping, 'carrying the 'seed, *
   will come again with 'jöy, 'shouldering their 'sheaves.

Psalm 127 *Nisi Dominus*

314 *R.H. Stanley*

315 *C. Hylton Stewart*

1 Unless the LORD ˈbuilds the ˈhouse, *
   their ˈlabor is in ˈvain who ˈbuild it.

2 Unless the LORD watches ˈover the ˈcity, *
   in vain the ˈwatchman ˈkeeps his ˈvigil.

3 It is in vain that you rise so early and go to ˈbed so ˈlate; *
   vain, too, to eat the bread of toil,
   for he gives to ˈhis beˈlovèd ˈsleep.

4 Children are a ˈheritage from the ˈLORD, *
   and the ˈfruit of the ˈwomb is a ˈgift.

5 Like arrows in the ˈhand of a ˈwarrior *
   are the ˈchildren of ˈone's ˈyouth.

6 Happy is the man who has his ˈquiver ˈfull of them! *
   he shall not be put to shame
   when he contends with his ˈenemies ˈin the ˈgate.

Psalm 128 *Beati omnes*

316   David Hurd

317   Hezekiah West

1 Happy are they all who 'fear the 'LORD, *
   and who 'follow 'in his 'ways!

2 You shall eat the 'fruit of your 'labor; *
   happiness and pros'perity 'shall be 'yours.

3 Your wife shall be like a fruitful vine with'in your 'house, *
   your children like olive shoots 'round a'bout your 'table.

4 The man who 'fears the 'LORD *
   shall 'thus in'deed be 'blessed.

5 The LORD 'bless you from 'Zion, *
   and may you see the prosperity of Jerusalem 'all the 'days of your 'life.

6 May you live to see your 'children's 'children; *
   may 'peace be up'ön 'Israel.

Psalm 129   *Saepe expugnaverunt*

318

Richard Clark

319

Cambridge Chant

1 "Greatly have they op'pressed me since my'youth," *
   let'Israel'nŏw'say;

2 "Greatly have they op'pressed me since my'youth, *
   but they'have not pre'vailed a'gainst me."

3 The plowmen'plowed upon my'back *
   and'made their'furrows'long.

4 The'LORD, the'Righteous One, *
   has'cut the'cords of the'wicked.

5 Let them be put to shame and'thrŏwn'back, *
   all'those who are'enemies of'Zion.

6 Let them be like'grass upon the'housetops, *
   which withers be'fore it'can be'plucked;

7 Which does not fill the'hand of the'reaper, *
   nor the bosom of'him who'binds the'sheaves;

8 So that those who go by say not as much as,
   "The'LŎRD'prosper you. *
   We wish you'well in the'Name of the'LORD."

Psalm 130   *De profundis*

320

C. Hylton Stewart

321

Henry Walford Davies

1 Out of the depths have I called to you, O LORD;
LORD,ˈhear myˈvoice; *
    let your ears consider well theˈvoice of myˈsuppliˈcation.

2 If you, LORD, were to note what isˈdone aˈmiss, *
    OˈLörd,ˈwho couldˈstand?

†3 For there is forˈgiveness withˈyou; *
    —ˈtherefore youˈshall beˈfeared.

4 I wait for the LORD; myˈsöulˈwaits for him; *
    in hisˈwördˈis myˈhope.

5 My soul waits for the LORD,
more thanˈwatchmen for theˈmorning, *
    more thanˈwatchmenˈfor theˈmorning.

6 O Israel,ˈwait for theˈLORD, *
    for with theˈLÖrdˈthere isˈmercy;

7 With him there isˈplenteous reˈdemption, *
    and he shall redeemˈIsrael fromˈall theirˈsins.

Psalm 131   *Domine, non est*

322   *John Goss*

323   *Benjamin Hutto*

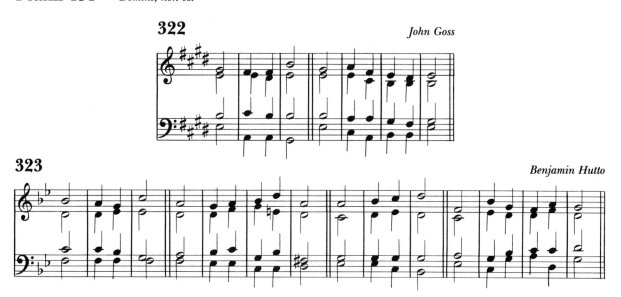

1 O LORD, I'am not'proud; *
    I'have no'haughty'looks.

2 I do not occupy myself with'grëat'matters, *
    or with'things that'are too'hard for me.

3 But I still my soul and make it quiet,
    like a child upon its'mother's'breast; *
    my'soul is'quieted with'in me.

4 O Israel,'wait upon the'LORD, *
    from this time'forth for'ever'more.

297

Psalm 132   *Memento, Domine*

324   *William Crotch*

325   *Edwin Edwards*

1 LORD, re'member 'David, *
    and all the 'hardships 'he en'dured;

2 How he swore an 'oath to the 'LORD *
    and vowed a vow to the 'Mighty 'One of 'Jacob:

3 "I will not come under the 'roof of my 'house, *
    nor 'climb up 'into my 'bed;

4 I will not allow my 'eyes to 'sleep, *
    nor 'let my 'eyelids 'slumber;

†5 Until I find a 'place for the 'LORD, *
    a dwelling for the 'Mighty 'One of 'Jacob."

6 "The ark! We 'heard it was in 'Ephratah; *
    we 'found it in the 'fields of 'Jearim.

7 Let us go to 'Göd's 'dwelling place; *
    let us fall upon our 'knees be'fore his 'footstool."

8 Arise, O 'LORD, into your 'resting-place, *
    you and the 'ark 'of your 'strength.

9 Let your priests be 'clothed with 'righteousness; *
    let your faithful 'people 'sing with 'joy.

298

10 For your servant⌐David's⌐sake, *
     do not turn away the⌐face of⌐your A⌐nointed.

11 The LORD has sworn an⌐oath to⌐David; *
     in⌐truth, he⌐will not⌐break it:

12 "A son, the⌐fruit of your⌐body *
     will I⌐set up⌐on your⌐throne.

13 If your children keep my covenant
     and my testimonies that⌐I shall⌐teach them, *
     their children will sit upon your⌐throne for⌐ever⌐more."

14 For the LORD has⌐chosen⌐Zion; *
     he has de⌐sired her for his⌐habi⌐tation:

15 "This shall be my⌐resting-place for⌐ever; *
     here will I⌐dwell, for⌐I de⌐light in her.

16 I will surely⌐bless her pro⌐visions, *
     and⌐satisfy her⌐poor with⌐bread.

17 I will clothe her⌐priests with sal⌐vation, *
     and her faithful⌐people will re⌐joice and⌐sing.

18 There will I make the horn of⌐David⌐flourish; *
     I have prepared a⌐lamp for⌐my A⌐nointed.

19 As for his enemies, I will⌐clothe them with⌐shame; *
     but as for⌐him, his⌐crown will⌐shine."

Psalm 133   *Ecce, quam bonum!*

326   *Richard Farrant*

327   *Gerre Hancock*

1 Oh, how good and |pleasant it |is, *
  when brethren |live to|gether in |unity!

2 It is like fine |oil upon the |head *
  that runs |down up|on the |beard,

†3 Upon the |beard of |Aaron, *
   and runs down upon the |collar |of his |robe.

4 It is like the |dew of |Hermon *
  that |falls upon the |hills of |Zion.

5 For there the LORD has or|dained the |blessing: *
  — |life for |ever|more.

Psalm 134   *Ecce nunc*

328   *Thomas Tallis* **329**   *Philip Tordoff*

1 Behold now, bless the LORD, all you |servants of the |LORD, *
  you that stand by |night in the |house of the |LORD.

2 Lift up your hands in the holy place and 'bless the 'LORD; *
   the LORD who made heaven and earth 'bless you 'out of 'Zion.

Psalm 135   *Laudate nomen*

330   *John Goss*

331   *Joseph Pring*

1 Hallelujah!
   Praise the 'Name of the 'LORD; *
      give praise, you 'servants 'of the 'LORD,

2 You who stand in the 'house of the 'LORD, *
      in the 'courts of the 'house of our 'God.

3 Praise the LORD, for the 'LORD is 'good; *
      sing praises to his 'Name, for 'it is 'lovely.

4 For the LORD has chosen 'Jacob for him 'self *
      and 'Israel for his 'own pos 'session.

†5 For I know that the 'LORD is 'great, *
      and that our 'Lord is a 'bove all 'gods.

6 The LORD does whatever pleases him, in 'heaven and on 'earth, *
      in the 'seas and 'all the 'deeps.

7 He brings up rain clouds from the 'ends of the 'earth; *
      he sends out lightning with the rain,
      and brings the 'winds 'out of his 'storehouse.

301

330

John Goss

331

Joseph Pring

8 It was he who struck down the ˈfirstborn of ˈEgypt, *
   the firstborn ˈboth of ˈman and ˈbeast.

9 He sent signs and wonders into the midst of ˈyou, O ˈEgypt, *
   against ˈPharaoh and ˈall his ˈservants.

10 He over ˈthrew many ˈnations *
   and put ˈmighty ˈkings to ˈdeath:

11 Sihon, king of the Amorites,
   and Og, the ˈking of ˈBashan, *
   and ˈall the ˈkingdoms of ˈCanaan.

†12 He gave their land to ˈbe an in ˈheritance, *
   an inheritance for ˈIsra ˈel his ˈpeople.

13 O LORD, your Name is ˈever ˈlasting; *
   your renown, O LORD, en ˈdures from ˈage to ˈage.

14 For the LORD gives his ˈpeople ˈjustice *
   and shows com ˈpassion ˈto his ˈservants.

15 The idols of the heathen are ˈsilver and ˈgold, *
   the ˈwork of ˈhuman ˈhands.

16 They have mouths, but they ˈcannot ˈspeak; *
   eyes have they, ˈbut they ˈcannot ˈsee.

17 They have ears, but they ˈcannot ˈhear; *
   neither is there ˈany ˈbreath in their ˈmouth.

18 Those who'make them are'like them, *
    and so are'all who'put their'trust in them.

19 Bless the LORD, O'house of'Israel; *
    O house of'Aaron,'bless the'LORD.

20 Bless the LORD, O'house of'Levi; *
    you who fear the'LÖRD,'bless the'LORD.

†21 Blessèd be the'LORD out of'Zion, *
    who dwells in Je'rusalem.'
    Halle'lujah!

Psalm 136 *Confitemini*

332

Thomas Norris

333

Alec Wyton

1 Give thanks to the'LORD, for he is'good, *
    for his'mercy en'dures for'ever.

2 Give thanks to the'God of'gods, *
    for his'mercy en'dures for'ever.

†3 Give thanks to the'Lord of'lords, *
    for his'mercy en'dures for'ever.

4 Who only'does great'wonders, *
    for his'mercy en'dures for'ever;

5 Who by'wisdom made the'heavens, *
    for his'mercy en'dures for'ever;

332

Thomas Norris

333

Alec Wyton

6 Who spread out the ⌐earth upon the⌐waters, *
  for his⌐mercy en⌐dures for⌐ever;

7 Who created⌐grëat⌐lights, *
  for his⌐mercy en⌐dures for⌐ever;

8 The sun to⌐rule the⌐day, *
  for his⌐mercy en⌐dures for⌐ever;

9 The moon and the stars to⌐govern the⌐night, *
  for his⌐mercy en⌐dures for⌐ever.

10 Who struck down the⌐firstborn of⌐Egypt, *
  for his⌐mercy en⌐dures for⌐ever;

11 And brought out⌐Israel from a⌐mong them, *
  for his⌐mercy en⌐dures for⌐ever;

†12 With a mighty hand and a⌐stretched-out⌐arm, *
  for his⌐mercy en⌐dures for⌐ever;

13 Who divided the Red⌐Sea in⌐two, *
  for his⌐mercy en⌐dures for⌐ever;

14 And made Israel to⌐pass through the⌐midst of it, *
  for his⌐mercy en⌐dures for⌐ever;

15 But swept Pharaoh and his army into the ˈRẽdˈSea, *
  for hisˈmercy enˈdures forˈever;

16 Who led hisˈpeople through theˈwilderness, *
  for hisˈmercy enˈdures forˈever.

17 Who struck downˈgrẽatˈkings, *
  for hisˈmercy enˈdures forˈever;

18 And slewˈmightyˈkings, *
  for hisˈmercy enˈdures forˈever;

19 Sihon,ˈking of theˈAmorites, *
  for hisˈmercy enˈdures forˈever;

20 And Og, theˈking ofˈBashan, *
  for hisˈmercy enˈdures forˈever;

21 And gave away theirˈlands for an inˈheritance, *
  for hisˈmercy enˈdures forˈever;

22 An inheritance forˈIsrael hisˈservant, *
  for hisˈmercy enˈdures forˈever.

23 Who remembered us in ourˈlow esˈtate, *
  for hisˈmercy enˈdures forˈever;

24 And deˈlivered us from ourˈenemies, *
  for hisˈmercy enˈdures forˈever;

25 Who givesˈfood to allˈcreatures, *
  for hisˈmercy enˈdures forˈever.

26 Give thanks to theˈGod ofˈheaven, *
  for hisˈmercy enˈdures forˈever.

Psalm 137 *Super flumina*

334   *Edwin George Monk*

335   *George Mursell Garrett*

1 By the waters of Babylon we sat⁣'down and⁣'wept, *
  when we re⁣'membered⁣'you, O⁣'Zion.

2 As for our harps, we⁣'hung them⁣'up *
  on the⁣'trees in the⁣'midst of that⁣'land.

3 For those who led us away captive asked us for a song,
  and our oppressors⁣'called for⁣'mirth: *
  "Sing us⁣'one of the⁣'songs of⁣'Zion."

4 How shall we⁣'sing the⁣'LORD's song *
  up⁣'on an⁣'alien⁣'soil?

5 If I forget you,⁣'O Je⁣'rusalem, *
  let my right⁣'hand for⁣'get its⁣'skill.

6 Let my tongue cleave to the roof of my mouth
  if I do⁣'not re⁣'member you, *
  if I do not set Jerusalem a⁣'bove my⁣'highest⁣'joy.

7 Remember the day of Jerusalem, O LORD,
  against the ˈpeople of ˈEdom, *
    who said, "Down with it! down with it!
    ˈeven ˈto the ˈground!"

8 O Daughter of Babylon, ˈdoomed to deˈstruction, *
  happy the one who pays you back
  for ˈwhat you have ˈdone to ˈus!

†9 Happy shall he be who ˈtakes your ˈlittle ones, *
   and ˈdashes them aˈgainst the ˈrock!

Psalm 138   *Confitebor tibi*

336   *Henry Dibdin*

337   *Henry Walford Davies*

1 I will give thanks to you, O LORD, with my ˈwhöle ˈheart; *
  before the ˈgods I will ˈsing your ˈpraise.

2 I will bow down toward your holy temple
  and ˈpraise your ˈName, *
    beˈcause of your ˈlove and ˈfaithfulness;

†3 For you have ˈglorified your ˈName *
   —ˈand your ˈword above ˈall things.

4 When I ˈcalled, you ˈanswered me; *
  you inˈcreased my ˈstrength withˈin me.

5 All the kings of the earth will ˈpraise you, O ˈLORD, *
  when they have ˈheard the ˈwords of your ˈmouth.

336

Henry Dibdin

337

Henry Walford Davies

6 They will sing of the ⌐ways of the⌐LORD, *
  that great is the⌐glory⌐of the⌐LORD.

7 Though the LORD be high, he⌐cares for the⌐lowly; *
  he perceives the⌐haughty⌐from a⌐far.

8 Though I walk in the midst of trouble, you⌐keep me⌐safe; *
  you stretch forth your hand against the fury of my enemies;
  ⌐your right⌐hand shall⌐save me.

9 The LORD will make good his⌐purpose for⌐me; *
  O LORD, your love endures for ever;
  do not a⌐bandon the⌐works of your⌐hands.

Psalm 139   *Domine, probasti*

338   *Samuel Sebastian Wesley*

339   *Charles Hubert Hastings Parry*

1   LORD, you have searched me'out and'known me; *
    you know my sitting down and my rising up;
    you dis'cern my'thoughts from a'far.

2   You trace my'journeys and my'resting-places *
    and are ac'quainted with'all my'ways.

3   Indeed, there is not a'word on my'lips, *
    but you, O LORD,'know it'alto'gether.

4   You press upon me be'hind and be'fore *
    and'lay your'hand up'on me.

†5 Such knowledge is too'wonderful for'me; *
    it is so'high that I'cannot at'tain to it.

6   Where can I go then'from your'Spirit? *
    where can I'flëe'from your'presence?

7   If I climb up to heaven,'you are'there; *
    if I make the grave my'bed, you are'thëre'also.

8   If I take the'wings of the'morning *
    and dwell in the'uttermost'parts of the'sea,

9   Even there your'hand will'lead me *
    and your'right hand'hold me'fast.

338

Samuel Sebastian Wesley

339

Charles Hubert Hastings Parry

10 If I say, "Surely the|darkness will|cover me, *
   and the light a|round me|turn to|night,"

11 Darkness is not dark to you;
   the night is as|bright as the|day; *
   darkness and light to|you are|both a|like.

12 For you yourself created my|inmost|parts; *
   you knit me to|gether in my|mother's|womb.

13 I will thank you because I am|marvelously|made; *
   your works are wonderful,|and I|know it|well.

14 My body was not|hidden from|you, *
   while I was being made in secret
   and|woven in the|depths of the|earth.

15 Your eyes beheld my limbs, yet unfinished in the womb;
   all of them were|written in your|book; *
   they were fashioned day by day,
   when as|yët|there was|none of them.

16 How deep I find your ' thoughts, O ' God! *
     how ' grëat ' is the ' sum of them!

17 If I were to count them, they would be more
               in ' number than the ' sand; *
     to count them all, my life span would ' need to ' be like ' yours.

18 Oh, that you would slay the ' wicked, O ' God! *
     You that ' thirst for ' blood, de ' part from me.

19 They speak de ' spitefully a ' gainst you; *
     your enemies ' take your ' Name in ' vain.

20 Do I not hate those, O ' LORD, who ' hate you? *
     and do I not loathe ' those who rise ' up a ' gainst you?

21 I hate them with a ' perfect ' hatred; *
     they have be ' come my ' öwn ' enemies.

22 Search me out, O God, and ' know my ' heart; *
     try me and ' know my ' restless ' thoughts.

23 Look well whether there be any ' wickedness ' in me *
     and lead me in the ' way that is ' ever ' lasting.

Psalm 140   *Eripe me, Domine*

340   *Sydney Nicholson*

341   *Joseph Barnby*

1 Deliver me, O LORD, from ‖ evil ‖ doers; *
   pro ‖ tect me ‖ from the ‖ violent.

2 Who devise ‖ evil in their ‖ hearts *
   and stir up ‖ strife ‖ all day ‖ long.

3 They have sharpened their ‖ tongues like a ‖ serpent; *
   adder's ‖ poison is ‖ under their ‖ lips.

4 Keep me, O LORD, from the ‖ hands of the ‖ wicked; *
   protect me from the violent,
   who are de ‖ termined to ‖ trip me ‖ up.

5 The proud have hidden a snare for me
   and stretched out a ‖ net of ‖ cords; *
   they have set ‖ traps for me a ‖ long the ‖ path.

6 I have said to the LORD, ‖ "You are my ‖ God; *
   listen, O ‖ LORD, to my ‖ suppli ‖ cation.

7 O Lord GOD, the strength of ‖ my sal ‖ vation, *
   you have covered my ‖ head in the ‖ day of ‖ battle.

8 Do not grant the desires of the ‖ wicked, O ‖ LORD, *
   nor let their ‖ evil ‖ pläns ‖ prosper.

9 Let not those who surround me lift'up their'heads; *
   let the'evil of their'lips over'whelm them.

10 Let hot burning'coals fall up'on them; *
   let them be cast into the mire, never to'rise'up a'gain."

11 A slanderer shall not be es'tablished on the'earth, *
   and'evil shall'hunt down the'lawless.

12 I know that the LORD will maintain the'cause of the'poor *
   and render'justice'to the'needy.

†13 Surely, the righteous will give'thanks to your'Name, *
   and the upright shall con'tinue'in your'sight.

Psalm 141 *Domine, clamavi*

342

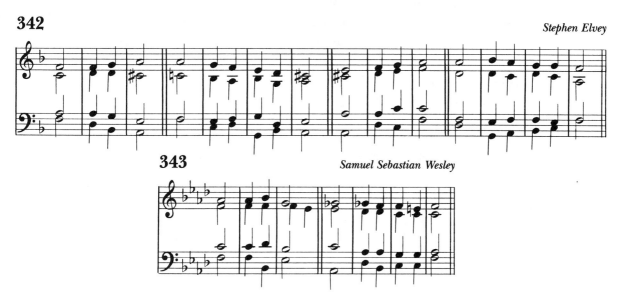

Stephen Elvey

343

Samuel Sebastian Wesley

1 O LORD, I call to you;'come to me'quickly; *
   hear my'voice'when I'cry to you.

2 Let my prayer be set forth in your'sight as'incense, *
   the lifting up of my'hands as the'evening'sacrifice.

3 Set a watch before my mouth, O LORD,
   and guard the'door of my'lips; *
   let not my heart incline to'any'evil'thing.

4 Let me not be occupied in wickedness with'evil'doers, *
   nor'eat of their'choice'foods.

342

Stephen Elvey

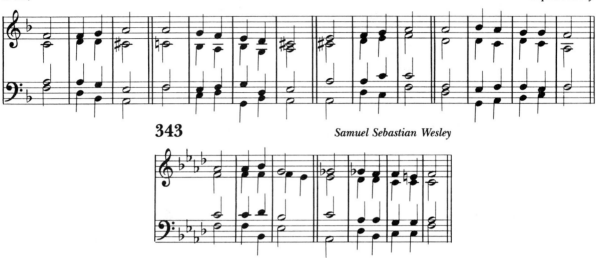

343

Samuel Sebastian Wesley

5 Let the righteous smite me in friendly rebuke;
   let not the oil of the unrighteous a'noint my'head; *
      for my prayer is continually a'gainst their'wicked'deeds.

6 Let their rulers be overthrown in'stony'places, *
      that they may'know my'words are'true.

7 As when a plowman turns over the'earth in'furrows, *
      let their bones be'scattered at the'mouth of the'grave.

8 But my eyes are turned to'you, Lord'GOD; *
      in you I take refuge;
      do not'strip me'of my'life.

9 Protect me from the snare which'they have'laid for me *
      and from the'traps of the'evil'doers.

10 Let the wicked fall into their'own'nets, *
      while'I my'self es'cape.

Psalm 142
Voce mea ad Dominum

344   *John Blow*   **345**   *C. Hylton Stewart*

1 I cry to the 'LORD with my 'voice; *
    to the LORD I make 'loüd 'suppli'cation.

2 I pour out my com'plaint be'fore him *
    and 'tell him 'all my 'trouble.

3 When my spirit languishes within me, you 'know my 'path; *
    in the way wherein I walk they have 'hidden a 'trap for 'me.

4 I look to my right hand and find 'no one who 'knows me; *
    I have no place to 'flee to, and 'no one 'cares for me.

5 I cry out to 'you, O 'LORD; *
    I say, "You are my refuge,
    my 'portion in the 'land of the 'living."

6 Listen to my cry for help, for I have been 'brought very 'low; *
    save me from those who pursue me,
    for 'they are too 'strong for 'me.

7 Bring me out of prison, that I may give 'thanks to your 'Name; *
    when you have dealt bountifully with me,
    the 'righteous will 'gather a 'round me.

346   *Samuel Wesley*

347   *Paul C. Edwards*

1 LORD, hear my prayer,
   and in your faithfulness heed my ' suppli ' cations; *
   answer ' më ' in your ' righteousness.

2 Enter not into ' judgment with your ' servant, *
   for in your sight shall ' no one ' living be ' justified.

†3 For my enemy has sought my life;
   he has ' crushed me to the ' ground; *
   he has made me live in dark places like ' those who are ' löng ' dead.

4 My spirit ' faints with ' in me; *
   my ' heart with ' in me is ' desolate.

5 I remember the time past;
   I muse upon ' all your ' deeds; *
   I con ' sider the ' works of your ' hands.

6 I spread ' out my ' hands to you; *
   my soul gasps to ' you like a ' thirsty ' land.

7 O LORD, make haste to answer me; my ˈspirit ˈfails me; *
  do not hide your face from me
  or I shall be like ˈthose who go ˈdown to the ˈPit.

8 Let me hear of your loving-kindness in the morning,
  for I ˈput my ˈtrust in you; *
    show me the road that I must walk,
    for ˈI lift ˈup my ˈsoul to you.

9 Deliver me from my ˈenemies, O ˈLORD, *
    for I ˈflee to ˈyou for ˈrefuge.

10 Teach me to do what pleases you, for ˈyou are my ˈGod; *
    let your good Spirit ˈlead me on ˈlevel ˈground.

11 Revive me, O ˈLORD, for your ˈName's sake; *
    for your righteousness' sake, ˈbring me ˈout of ˈtrouble.

†12 Of your goodness, destroy my enemies
  and bring all my ˈfoes to ˈnaught, *
    for ˈtruly ˈI am your ˈservant.

Psalm 144   *Benedictus Dominus*

348

Thomas Jackson

349

Herbert Hall Woodward

1 Blessèd be the 'LORD my 'rock! *
   who trains my hands to 'fight and my 'fingers to 'battle;

2 My help and my fortress, my stronghold and 'my de'liverer, *
   my shield in whom I trust,
   who sub'dues the 'peoples 'under me.

3 O LORD, what are we that 'you should 'care for us? *
   mere 'mortals that 'you should 'think of us?

4 We are like a 'puff of 'wind; *
   our days are 'like a 'passing 'shadow.

5 Bow your heavens, O 'LORD, and come 'down; *
   touch the 'mountains, and 'they shall 'smoke.

6 Hurl the 'lightning and 'scatter them; *
   shoot 'out your 'arrows and 'rout them.

7 Stretch out your 'hand from on 'high; *
   rescue me and deliver me from the great waters,
   from the 'hand of 'foreign 'peoples,

8 Whose mouths 'speak de'ceitfully *
   and whose right 'hand is 'raised in 'falsehood.

9 O God, I will sing to you a ' new ' song; *
   I will play to ' you on a ' ten-stringed ' lyre.

10 You give ' victory to ' kings *
   and have ' rescued ' David your ' servant.

11 Rescue me from the ' hurtful ' sword *
   and deliver me from the ' hand of ' foreign ' peoples,

12 Whose mouths ' speak de ' ceitfully *
   and whose right ' hand is ' raised in ' falsehood.

13 May our sons be like plants well ' nurtured from their ' youth, *
   and our daughters like sculptured ' corners ' of a ' palace.

14 May our barns be filled to overflowing with all ' manner of ' crops; *
   may the flocks in our pastures increase by thousands and
                tens of thousands;
   may our ' cattle be ' fat and ' sleek.

15 May there be no breaching of the walls, no ' going into ' exile, *
   no ' wailing in the ' public ' squares.

16 Happy are the people of whom ' this is ' so! *
   happy are the ' people whose ' God is the ' LORD!

Psalm 145 *Exaltabo te, Deus*

350 *Joseph Barnby*

351 *William Marsh*

1 I will exalt you, O ' God my ' King, *
    and bless your ' Name for ' ever and ' ever.

2 Every ' day will I ' bless you *
    and praise your ' Name for ' ever and ' ever.

3 Great is the LORD and ' greatly to be ' praised; *
    there ' is no ' end to his ' greatness.

4 One generation shall praise your ' works to an ' other *
    and ' shall de ' clare your ' power.

5 I will ponder the glorious ' splendor of your ' majesty *
    and ' all your ' marvelous ' works.

6 They shall speak of the might of your ' wondrous ' acts, *
    and ' I will ' tell of your ' greatness.

7 They shall publish the remembrance of your ' grëat ' goodness; *
    they shall ' sing of your ' righteous ' deeds.

8 The LORD is gracious and ' full of com ' passion, *
    slow to ' anger and of ' grëat ' kindness.

9 The LORD is ꞌloving to ꞌeveryone *
    and his compassion is ꞌover ꞌall his ꞌworks.

10 All your works ꞌpraise you, O ꞌLORD, *
    and your ꞌfaithful ꞌservants ꞌbless you.

11 They make known the ꞌglory of your ꞌkingdom *
    and ꞌspëak ꞌof your ꞌpower;

12 That the peoples may ꞌknow of your ꞌpower *
    and the glorious ꞌsplendor ꞌof your ꞌkingdom.

13 Your kingdom is an ever ꞌlasting ꞌkingdom; *
    your dominion en ꞌdures through ꞌout all ꞌages.

14 The LORD is faithful in ꞌall his ꞌwords *
    and ꞌmerciful in ꞌall his ꞌdeeds.

15 The LORD upholds all ꞌthose who ꞌfall; *
    he lifts up ꞌthose who are ꞌböwed ꞌdown.

16 The eyes of all wait upon ꞌyou, O ꞌLORD, *
    and you give them their ꞌfood in ꞌdüe ꞌseason.

17 You open ꞌwide your ꞌhand *
    and satisfy the needs of ꞌevery ꞌliving ꞌcreature.

18 The LORD is righteous in ꞌall his ꞌways *
    and ꞌloving in ꞌall his ꞌworks.

19 The LORD is near to those who ꞌcall up ꞌon him, *
    to all who ꞌcall up ꞌon him ꞌfaithfully.

20 He fulfills the desire of ꞌthose who ꞌfear him; *
    he ꞌhears their ꞌcry and ꞌhelps them.

21 The LORD preserves all ꞌthose who ꞌlove him, *
    but he de ꞌströys ꞌall the ꞌwicked.

22 My mouth shall speak the ꞌpraise of the ꞌLORD; *
    let all flesh bless his holy ꞌName for ꞌever and ꞌever.

Psalm 146 *Lauda, anima mea*

352

Thomas Norris

353

Edward Cuthbert Bairstow

1 Hallelujah!
  Praise the LORD,'O my'soul! *
    I will praise the LORD as long as I live;
    I will sing praises to my'God while I'have my'being.

2 Put not your trust in rulers, nor in any'child of'earth, *
    —'for there'is no'help in them.

3 When they breathe their last, they re'turn to'earth, *
    and in that'day their'thoughts'perish.

4 Happy are they who have the God of'Jacob for their'help! *
    whose'hope is in the'LORD their'God;

5 Who made heaven and earth, the seas, and'all that is'in them; *
    who'keeps his'promise for'ever;

6 Who gives justice to'those who are op'pressed, *
    and'food to'those who'hunger.

7 The LORD sets the prisoners free;
    the LORD opens the'eyes of the'blind; *
    the LORD lifts up'those who are'bowed'down;

322

8 The LORD loves the righteous;
  the LORD ' cares for the ' stranger; *
    he sustains the orphan and widow,
    but ' frustrates the ' way of the ' wicked.

†9 The LORD shall ' reign for ' ever, *
  your God, O Zion, throughout all gene ' rations. '
  Halle ' lujah!

Psalm 147 *Laudate Dominum*

354

Frederick A. Gore Ouseley

355

George Thalben-Ball

1 Hallelujah!
  How good it is to sing ' praises to our ' God! *
    how pleasant it is to ' honor ' him with ' praise!

2 The LORD re ' builds Je ' rusalem; *
  he ' gathers the ' exiles of ' Israel.

3 He heals the ' broken ' hearted *
  and ' binds ' up their ' wounds.

4 He counts the ' number of the ' stars *
  and ' calls them ' all by their ' names.

5 Great is our LORD and ' mighty in ' power; *
  there is no ' limit ' to his ' wisdom.

6 The LORD lifts ' up the ' lowly, *
  but casts the ' wicked ' to the ' ground.

354

Frederick A. Gore Ouseley

355

George Thalben-Ball

7 Sing to the 'LORD with 'thanksgiving; *
   make music to our 'God up'on the 'harp.

8 He covers the 'heavens with 'clouds *
   and pre'päres 'rain for the 'earth;

†9 He makes grass to 'grow upon the 'mountains *
   and green 'plants to 'serve man'kind.

10 He provides food for 'flocks and 'herds *
   and for the young 'ravens 'when they 'cry.

11 He is not impressed by the 'might of a 'horse; *
   he has no 'pleasure in the 'strength of a 'man;

†12 But the LORD has pleasure in 'those who 'fear him, *
   in those who a'wait his 'gracious 'favor.

13 Worship the LORD, 'O Je'rusalem; *
   — 'praise your 'God, O 'Zion;

14 For he has strengthened the 'bars of your 'gates; *
   he has 'blessed your 'children with'in you.

15 He has established 'peace on your 'borders; *
   he satisfies you 'with the 'finest 'wheat.

16 He sends out his com'mand to the 'earth, *
   and his 'word runs 'very 'swiftly.

17 He gives ' snow like ' wool; *
    he ' scatters ' hoarfrost like ' ashes.

18 He scatters his ' hail like ' bread crumbs; *
    who can ' stand a ' gainst his ' cold?

†19 He sends forth his ' word and ' melts them; *
    he blows with his ' wind, and the ' waters ' flow.

20 He declares his ' word to ' Jacob, *
    his ' statutes and his ' judgments to ' Israel.

21 He has not done so to ' any other ' nation; *
    to them he has not revealed his ' judgments. '
    Halle ' lujah!

Psalm 148   *Laudate Dominum*

356   *David Koehring*

357   *Thomas Attwood Walmisley*

1 Hallelujah!
  Praise the ˈLORD from the ˈheavens; *
    — ˈpraise him ˈin the ˈheights.

2 Praise him, ˈall you ˈangels of his; *
    — ˈpraise him, ˈall his ˈhost.

3 Praise him, ˈsun and ˈmoon; *
    praise him, ˈall you ˈshining ˈstars.

4 Praise him, ˈheaven of ˈheavens, *
    and you ˈwaters aˈbove the ˈheavens.

5 Let them praise the ˈName of the ˈLORD; *
    for he comˈmanded, and ˈthey were creˈated.

6 He made them stand fast for ˈever and ˈever; *
    he gave them a law which ˈshall not ˈpass aˈway.

7 Praise the ˈLORD from the ˈearth, *
    you ˈsea-monsters and ˈäll ˈdeeps;

8 Fire and hail, ˈsnow and ˈfog, *
    tempestuous ˈwind, ˈdoing his ˈwill;

9 Mountains and ᵃll ˈhills, *
— ˈfruit trees and ˈᵃll ˈcedars;

10 Wild beasts and ˈᵃll ˈcattle, *
creeping ˈthings and ˈwingèd ˈbirds;

11 Kings of the earth and ˈᵃll ˈpeoples, *
princes and all ˈrulers ˈof the ˈworld;

12 Young ˈmen and ˈmaidens, *
— ˈold and ˈyoung to ˈgether.

13 Let them praise the ˈName of the ˈLORD, *
for his Name only is exalted,
his splendor is ˈover ˈearth and ˈheaven.

14 He has raised up strength for his people
and praise for all his ˈloyal ˈservants, *
the children of Israel, a people who are ˈnear him. ˈ
ˈHalle ˈlujah!

Psalm 149   *Cantate Domino*

358   *Henry Smart*

359   *John Barnard*

1 Hallelujah!
   Sing to the LORD a'nĕw'song; *
     sing his praise in the congre'gation'of the'faithful.

2 Let Israel re'joice in his'Maker; *
     let the children of Zion be'joyful'in their'King.

3 Let them praise his'Name in the'dance; *
     let them sing'praise to him with'timbrel and'harp.

4 For the LORD takes'pleasure in his'people *
     and a'dorns the'poor with'victory.

5 Let the faithful re'joice in'triumph; *
     let them be'joyful'on their'beds.

6 Let the praises of'God be in their'throat *
     and a'two-edged'sword in their'hand;

7 To wreak'vengeance on the'nations *
     and'punishment'on the'peoples;

8 To bind their'kings in'chains *
     and their'nobles with'links of'iron;

†9 To inflict on them the'judgment de'creed; *
     this is glory for all his faithful'people.'
     Halle'lujah!

Psalm 150   *Laudate Dominum*

360

John Goss

1 Hallelujah!
  Praise God in his 'holy 'temple; *
    praise him in the 'firmament 'of his 'power.

2 Praise him for his 'mighty 'acts; *
    praise him 'for his 'excellent 'greatness.

3 Praise him with the 'blast of the 'ram's-horn; *
    — 'praise him with 'lyre and 'harp.

4 Praise him with 'timbrel and 'dance; *
    — 'praise him with 'strings and 'pipe.

5 Praise him with re 'sounding 'cymbals; *
    praise him with 'loüd 'clanging 'cymbals.

6 Let everything 'that has 'breath *
    praise the 'LORD. '
    'Halle 'lujah!

Psalm 150

361

Charles Villiers Stanford

f Unison

Hallelujah! Praise God in his ho - ly tem - ple;* praise him in the fir-ma-ment of his power.

2. Praise him for his might - y acts;*___ praise him for his ex - cel -lent greatness.

Harmony

3. Praise him with the blast of the ram's horn;* praise him with lyre and harp.

4. Praise him with tim - brel and dance;*___ praise him with strings and pipe.

Indexes

Copyright Acknowledgments

Index of Chants

Single Chants

Note: Upper case letters indicate major key, lower case indicates minor. An asterisk indicates a transposition of the previous chant.

Composer or Source	Key	Number
Battishill, Jonathan (1738–1801)	C	246
Blow, John (1649?–1708)	d	75, 115, 250, 279, 344
Brown, Ray Francis (1897–1965)	E	61
	F	218, 265
	F	249
Burgomaster, Frederick (b. 1941)	a	157
Coleman, Richard H. Pinwill (b. 1888)	B♭	31, 112
Cooke, Benjamin (1734–1793)	E	254
Davies, Henry Walford (1869–1941)	a	113, 183, 307
	A	114
Elgar, Edward William (1857–1934)	G	132
Elvey, Stephen (1805–1860)	A	253, 280
Farrant, Richard (1530–1580)	F	55, 310, 328
	D*	288
Goodson, Richard (1655?–1718)	C	130
Goss, John (1800–1880)	E	49, 281, 322
	f	11, 27
	G	117
Hancock, Gerre (b. 1932)	A	2
Harrison, Julius (1808–1871)	d	134
	D	135
Hesford, Bryan (b. 1930)	a	301
Hopkins, Edward John (1818–1901)	F	205
Hurd, David (b. 1950)	e	267
	F	152
	F	187
	F	316
	B♭	151
	B♭	304
Hurford, Peter (b. 1930)	E	311
Keys, Ivor (b. 1919)	E	15
Macfarren, George A. (1813–1887)	A♭	223
	a	156
Monk, Edwin George (1819–1900)	G	259
	f♯	289
	g*	284
	g	3, 334
	a	196
Nares, James (1715?–1783)	A	29
	F*	277
Nicholson, Sydney (1875–1947)	D	59, 212, 269, 340

Ouseley, Frederick A. Gore (1825–1909)	d	125
	D	126
	B♭	1, 278
Parisian Tone	E♭	283
	F*	25
Purcell, Henry (1659–1695)	g	123
	G	124
Rimbault, Edward (1816–1876)	D	286, 314
Savage, William (1720–1789)	C	247
Stainer, John (1840–1901)	B♭	76, 277, 273
Stanley, R. H.	G	285, 314
Stewart, C. Hylton (1884–1932)	c	118
	D	88, 173, 186, 282, 306
	g	21
	b	300, 320
	c*	345
Stewart, Robert P. (1825–1894)	C	184, 216, 252
Tallis, Thomas (1505?–1585)	B♭	225, 308, 328
	A*	287
Thalben-Ball, George (b. 1896)	a	148
Tordoff, Philip	F	274, 329
Wesley, Samuel Sebastian (1810–1876)	F	343

Double Chants

Composer or Source	Key	Number
Alcock, Walter Galpin (1861–1947)	E♭	161
Atkins, Ivor Algernon (1869–1953)	E♭	97
	E♭	159
	G	37
	B♭	58, 305
	B♭	224
Attwood, Thomas (1765–1838)	D	226
	G	264
	A♭	74
	B♭	251
Bairstow, Edward Cuthbert (1874–1946)	D	237
	E♭	32, 50
	F*	149, 353
	G	236
Barnard, John (b. 1948)	A♭	211, 359
Barnby, Joseph (1838–1896)	c	214
	d*	106
	E	350
	f♯	163
	a	66, 142
	A	341
	B♭	138
Battishill, Jonathan (1738–1801)	F	5, 107, 181
	a	137, 154

Woodward, Richard Jr. (1744–1777)	D	168
	A♭	70
Wyton, Alec (b. 1921)	C	243
	f	47, 244
	G	333
	A♭	239

Triple Chants

Composer or Source	Key	Number
Dirksen, Richard Wayne (b. 1921)	d	143
Naylor, John (1838–1897)	E♭	169
Stewart, C. Hylton (1884–1932)	D	170

Through-Composed Chant

Composer or Source	Key	Number
Stanford, Charles Villiers (1852–1924)	C	361